ThirdParty Management
Complete Self-Assessment Guide

The guidance in this Self-Assessment is based on ThirdParty Management best practices and standards in business process architecture, design and quality management. The guidance is also based on the professional judgment of the individual collaborators listed in the Acknowledgments.

Notice of rights

Trademarks

Table of Contents

About The Art of Service

The Art of Service, Business Process Architects since 2000, is dedicated to helping stakeholders achieve excellence.

Defining, designing, creating, and implementing a process to solve a stakeholders challenge or meet an objective is the most valuable role… In EVERY group, company, organization and department.

Unless you're talking a one-time, single-use project, there should be a process. Whether that process is managed and implemented by humans, AI, or a combination of the two, it needs to be designed by someone with a complex enough perspective to ask the right questions.

Someone capable of asking the right questions and step back and say, 'What are we really trying to accomplish here? And Is there a different way to look at it?'

With The Art of Service's Standard Requirements Self-Assessments, we empower people who can do just that — whether their title is marketer, entrepreneur, manager, salesperson, consultant, Business Process Manager, executive assistant, IT Manager, CIO etc... —they are the people who rule the future. They are people who watch the process as it happens, and ask the right questions to make the process work better.

Contact us when you need any support with this Self-Assessment and any help with templates, blue-prints and examples of standard documents you might need:

http://theartofservice.com
service@theartofservice.com

Acknowledgments

This checklist was developed under the auspices of The Art of Service, chaired by Gerardus Blokdyk.

Representatives from several client companies participated in the preparation of this Self-Assessment.

In addition, we are thankful for the design and printing services provided.

Included Resources - how to access

Included with your purchase of the book is the ThirdParty Management Self-Assessment Spreadsheet Dashboard which contains all questions and Self-Assessment areas and auto-generates insights, graphs, and project RACI planning - all with examples to get you started right away.

How? Simply send an email to
access@theartofservice.com
with this books' title in the subject to get the ThirdParty Management Self Assessment Tool right away.

You will receive the following contents with New and Updated specific criteria:

- The latest quick edition of the book in PDF

- The latest complete edition of the book in PDF, which criteria correspond to the criteria in...

- The Self-Assessment Excel Dashboard, and...

- Example pre-filled Self-Assessment Excel Dashboard to get familiar with results generation

- In-depth specific Checklists covering the topic

- Project management checklists and templates to assist with implementation

INCLUDES LIFETIME SELF ASSESSMENT UPDATES

Every self assessment comes with Lifetime Updates and Lifetime Free Updated Books. Lifetime Updates is an industry-first feature which allows you to receive verified self assessment updates, ensuring you always have the most accurate information at your fingertips.

Get it now- you will be glad you did - do it now, before you forget.

Send an email to **access@theartofservice.com** with this books' title in the subject to get the ThirdParty Management Self Assessment Tool right away.

Your feedback is invaluable to us

If you recently bought this book, we would love to hear from you! You can do this by writing a review on amazon (or the online store where you purchased this book) about your last purchase! As part of our continual service improvement process, we love to hear real client experiences and feedback.

How does it work?
To post a review on Amazon, just log in to your account and click on the Create Your Own Review button (under Customer Reviews) of the relevant product page. You can find examples of product reviews in Amazon. If you purchased from another online store, simply follow their procedures.

What happens when I submit my review?
Once you have submitted your review, send us an email at review@theartofservice.com with the link to your review so we can properly thank you for your feedback.

Purpose of this Self-Assessment

This Self-Assessment has been developed to improve understanding of the requirements and elements of ThirdParty Management, based on best practices and standards in business process architecture, design and quality management.

It is designed to allow for a rapid Self-Assessment to determine how closely existing management practices and procedures correspond to the elements of the Self-Assessment.

The criteria of requirements and elements of ThirdParty Management have been rephrased in the format of a Self-Assessment questionnaire, with a seven-criterion scoring system, as explained in this document.

In this format, even with limited background knowledge of

ThirdParty Management, a manager can quickly review existing operations to determine how they measure up to the standards. This in turn can serve as the starting point of a 'gap analysis' to identify management tools or system elements that might usefully be implemented in the organization to help improve overall performance.

How to use the Self-Assessment

On the following pages are a series of questions to identify to what extent your ThirdParty Management initiative is complete in comparison to the requirements set in standards.

To facilitate answering the questions, there is a space in front of each question to enter a score on a scale of '1' to '5'.

1 Strongly Disagree

2 Disagree

3 Neutral

4 Agree

5 Strongly Agree

Read the question and rate it with the following in front of mind:

'In my belief,
the answer to this question is clearly defined'.

There are two ways in which you can choose to interpret this statement;
1. how aware are you that the answer to the question is clearly defined
2. for more in-depth analysis you can choose to gather

evidence and confirm the answer to the question. This obviously will take more time, most Self-Assessment users opt for the first way to interpret the question and dig deeper later on based on the outcome of the overall Self-Assessment.

A score of '1' would mean that the answer is not clear at all, where a '5' would mean the answer is crystal clear and defined. Leave emtpy when the question is not applicable or you don't want to answer it, you can skip it without affecting your score. Write your score in the space provided.

After you have responded to all the appropriate statements in each section, compute your average score for that section, using the formula provided, and round to the nearest tenth. Then transfer to the corresponding spoke in the ThirdParty Management Scorecard on the second next page of the Self-Assessment.

Your completed ThirdParty Management Scorecard will give you a clear presentation of which ThirdParty Management areas need attention.

ThirdParty Management Scorecard Example

Example of how the finalized Scorecard can look like:

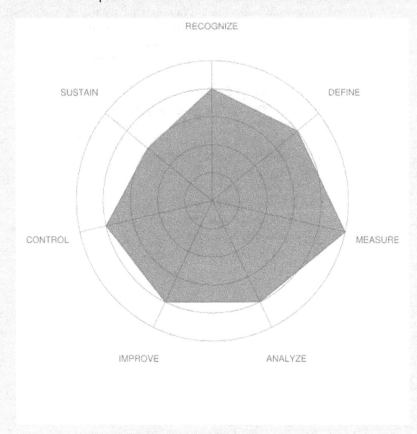

ThirdParty Management Scorecard

Your Scores:

BEGINNING OF THE
SELF-ASSESSMENT:

CRITERION #1: RECOGNIZE

INTENT: Be aware of the need for change. Recognize that there is an unfavorable variation, problem or symptom.

In my belief, the answer to this question is clearly defined:

5 Strongly Agree

4 Agree

3 Neutral

2 Disagree

1 Strongly Disagree

1. When a ThirdParty Management manager recognizes a problem, what options are available?
<--- Score

2. For your ThirdParty Management project, identify and describe the business environment, is there more than one layer to the business environment?
<--- Score

3. Do you recognize ThirdParty Management achievements?

<--- Score

4. Why is this needed?

<--- Score

5. How are training requirements identified?

<--- Score

6. What vendors make products that address the ThirdParty Management needs?

<--- Score

7. Think about the people you identified for your ThirdParty Management project and the project responsibilities you would assign to them, what kind of training do you think they would need to perform these responsibilities effectively?

<--- Score

8. Where do you need to exercise leadership?

<--- Score

9. Which needs are not included or involved?

<--- Score

10. Are there any specific expectations or concerns about the ThirdParty Management team, ThirdParty Management itself?

<--- Score

11. What do employees need in the short term?

<--- Score

12. Are your goals realistic? Do you need to redefine

your problem? Perhaps the problem has changed or maybe you have reached your goal and need to set a new one?

<--- Score

13. Who else hopes to benefit from it?

<--- Score

14. What should be considered when identifying available resources, constraints, and deadlines?

<--- Score

15. What is the problem or issue?

<--- Score

16. Do you know what you need to know about ThirdParty Management?

<--- Score

17. What problems are you facing and how do you consider ThirdParty Management will circumvent those obstacles?

<--- Score

18. What tools and technologies are needed for a custom ThirdParty Management project?

<--- Score

19. Do you need different information or graphics?

<--- Score

20. Which information does the ThirdParty Management business case need to include?

<--- Score

21. Are losses recognized in a timely manner?

<--- Score

22. Whom do you really need or want to serve?
<--- Score

23. What are the stakeholder objectives to be achieved with ThirdParty Management?
<--- Score

24. What is the smallest subset of the problem you can usefully solve?
<--- Score

25. What does ThirdParty Management success mean to the stakeholders?
<--- Score

26. How do you assess your ThirdParty Management workforce capability and capacity needs, including skills, competencies, and staffing levels?
<--- Score

27. How does it fit into your organizational needs and tasks?
<--- Score

28. Do you have/need 24-hour access to key personnel?
<--- Score

29. What ThirdParty Management events should you attend?
<--- Score

30. Consider your own ThirdParty Management project, what types of organizational problems do

you think might be causing or affecting your problem, based on the work done so far?
<--- Score

31. Will ThirdParty Management deliverables need to be tested and, if so, by whom?
<--- Score

32. How do you take a forward-looking perspective in identifying ThirdParty Management research related to market response and models?
<--- Score

33. What are the expected benefits of ThirdParty Management to the stakeholder?
<--- Score

34. Have you identified your ThirdParty Management key performance indicators?
<--- Score

35. Does ThirdParty Management create potential expectations in other areas that need to be recognized and considered?
<--- Score

36. Who needs to know about ThirdParty Management?
<--- Score

37. Will a response program recognize when a crisis occurs and provide some level of response?
<--- Score

38. What are the timeframes required to resolve each of the issues/problems?

<--- Score

39. What are the minority interests and what amount of minority interests can be recognized?
<--- Score

40. Do you need to avoid or amend any ThirdParty Management activities?
<--- Score

41. What is the recognized need?
<--- Score

42. Who needs what information?
<--- Score

43. Is it clear when you think of the day ahead of you what activities and tasks you need to complete?
<--- Score

44. Would you recognize a threat from the inside?
<--- Score

45. What ThirdParty Management problem should be solved?
<--- Score

46. Are there any revenue recognition issues?
<--- Score

47. Who should resolve the ThirdParty Management issues?
<--- Score

48. How do you recognize an objection?
<--- Score

49. As a sponsor, customer or management, how important is it to meet goals, objectives?
<--- Score

50. Which issues are too important to ignore?
<--- Score

51. Are employees recognized or rewarded for performance that demonstrates the highest levels of integrity?
<--- Score

52. Does the problem have ethical dimensions?
<--- Score

53. What prevents you from making the changes you know will make you a more effective ThirdParty Management leader?
<--- Score

54. How do you identify the kinds of information that you will need?
<--- Score

55. What ThirdParty Management capabilities do you need?
<--- Score

56. How are the ThirdParty Management's objectives aligned to the group's overall stakeholder strategy?
<--- Score

57. What resources or support might you need?
<--- Score

58. How do you recognize an ThirdParty Management objection?
<--- Score

59. Is the quality assurance team identified?
<--- Score

60. What are your needs in relation to ThirdParty Management skills, labor, equipment, and markets?
<--- Score

61. What do you need to start doing?
<--- Score

62. Who defines the rules in relation to any given issue?
<--- Score

63. How many trainings, in total, are needed?
<--- Score

64. Are you dealing with any of the same issues today as yesterday? What can you do about this?
<--- Score

65. What are the clients issues and concerns?
<--- Score

66. Are employees recognized for desired behaviors?
<--- Score

67. What creative shifts do you need to take?
<--- Score

68. What ThirdParty Management coordination do

you need?

<--- Score

69. What situation(s) led to this ThirdParty Management Self Assessment?

<--- Score

70. Can management personnel recognize the monetary benefit of ThirdParty Management?

<--- Score

71. Are there ThirdParty Management problems defined?

<--- Score

72. Who needs to know?

<--- Score

73. To what extent would your organization benefit from being recognized as a award recipient?

<--- Score

74. Who are your key stakeholders who need to sign off?

<--- Score

75. Is it needed?

<--- Score

76. What needs to stay?

<--- Score

77. What information do users need?

<--- Score

78. Are problem definition and motivation clearly

presented?
<--- Score

79. Why the need?
<--- Score

80. Where is training needed?
<--- Score

81. How are you going to measure success?
<--- Score

82. Are controls defined to recognize and contain problems?
<--- Score

83. What else needs to be measured?
<--- Score

84. What training and capacity building actions are needed to implement proposed reforms?
<--- Score

85. What would happen if ThirdParty Management weren't done?
<--- Score

86. What needs to be done?
<--- Score

87. What are the ThirdParty Management resources needed?
<--- Score

88. Did you miss any major ThirdParty Management issues?

<--- Score

89. Are there regulatory / compliance issues?
<--- Score

90. Looking at each person individually – does every one have the qualities which are needed to work in this group?
<--- Score

91. Does your organization need more ThirdParty Management education?
<--- Score

92. Is the need for organizational change recognized?
<--- Score

93. How do you identify subcontractor relationships?
<--- Score

94. How much are sponsors, customers, partners, stakeholders involved in ThirdParty Management? In other words, what are the risks, if ThirdParty Management does not deliver successfully?
<--- Score

Add up total points for this section:
_ _ _ _ _ = Total points for this section

Divided by: _ _ _ _ _ _ (number of statements answered) = _ _ _ _ _ _
Average score for this section

Transfer your score to the ThirdParty Management Index at the beginning of

the Self-Assessment.

CRITERION #2: DEFINE:

INTENT: Formulate the stakeholder problem. Define the problem, needs and objectives.

In my belief, the answer to this question is clearly defined:

5 Strongly Agree

4 Agree

3 Neutral

2 Disagree

1 Strongly Disagree

1. What scope do you want your strategy to cover?
<--- Score

2. What scope to assess?
<--- Score

3. What are the requirements for audit information?
<--- Score

4. Are resources adequate for the scope?
<--- Score

5. Has the ThirdParty Management work been fairly and/or equitably divided and delegated among team members who are qualified and capable to perform the work? Has everyone contributed?
<--- Score

6. Is the current 'as is' process being followed? If not, what are the discrepancies?
<--- Score

7. Are customer(s) identified and segmented according to their different needs and requirements?
<--- Score

8. Do the problem and goal statements meet the SMART criteria (specific, measurable, attainable, relevant, and time-bound)?
<--- Score

9. How often are the team meetings?
<--- Score

10. Is the improvement team aware of the different versions of a process: what they think it is vs. what it actually is vs. what it should be vs. what it could be?
<--- Score

11. Are roles and responsibilities formally defined?
<--- Score

12. Has your scope been defined?
<--- Score

13. Is the team adequately staffed with the desired cross-functionality? If not, what additional resources are available to the team?
<--- Score

14. Will team members perform ThirdParty Management work when assigned and in a timely fashion?
<--- Score

15. What constraints exist that might impact the team?
<--- Score

16. How have you defined all ThirdParty Management requirements first?
<--- Score

17. What sources do you use to gather information for a ThirdParty Management study?
<--- Score

18. What is the worst case scenario?
<--- Score

19. What key stakeholder process output measure(s) does ThirdParty Management leverage and how?
<--- Score

20. What customer feedback methods were used to solicit their input?
<--- Score

21. Do you have a ThirdParty Management success story or case study ready to tell and share?
<--- Score

22. What was the context?
<--- Score

23. How do you gather requirements?
<--- Score

24. Does the team have regular meetings?
<--- Score

25. How do you keep key subject matter experts in the loop?
<--- Score

26. What is the scope?
<--- Score

27. What is the scope of the ThirdParty Management work?
<--- Score

28. When is/was the ThirdParty Management start date?
<--- Score

29. Is special ThirdParty Management user knowledge required?
<--- Score

30. Is there a critical path to deliver ThirdParty Management results?
<--- Score

31. Who is gathering information?
<--- Score

32. What are the dynamics of the communication plan?
<--- Score

33. How would you define ThirdParty Management leadership?
<--- Score

34. How do you manage unclear ThirdParty Management requirements?
<--- Score

35. What is the definition of ThirdParty Management excellence?
<--- Score

36. What gets examined?
<--- Score

37. What is the context?
<--- Score

38. What is in the scope and what is not in scope?
<--- Score

39. What intelligence can you gather?
<--- Score

40. Is data collected and displayed to better understand customer(s) critical needs and requirements.
<--- Score

41. What would be the goal or target for a ThirdParty Management's improvement team?
<--- Score

42. How does the ThirdParty Management manager ensure against scope creep?
<--- Score

43. Who is gathering ThirdParty Management information?
<--- Score

44. Why are you doing ThirdParty Management and what is the scope?
<--- Score

45. How do you manage scope?
<--- Score

46. Is there a ThirdParty Management management charter, including stakeholder case, problem and goal statements, scope, milestones, roles and responsibilities, communication plan?
<--- Score

47. Is there regularly 100% attendance at the team meetings? If not, have appointed substitutes attended to preserve cross-functionality and full representation?
<--- Score

48. Have specific policy objectives been defined?
<--- Score

49. Is there any additional ThirdParty Management definition of success?
<--- Score

50. Are required metrics defined, what are they?

<--- Score

51. Are there any constraints known that bear on the ability to perform ThirdParty Management work? How is the team addressing them?
<--- Score

52. How do you hand over ThirdParty Management context?
<--- Score

53. Have the customer needs been translated into specific, measurable requirements? How?
<--- Score

54. When is the estimated completion date?
<--- Score

55. What is in scope?
<--- Score

56. How do you think the partners involved in ThirdParty Management would have defined success?
<--- Score

57. What are the boundaries of the scope? What is in bounds and what is not? What is the start point? What is the stop point?
<--- Score

58. Where can you gather more information?
<--- Score

59. Are there different segments of customers?
<--- Score

60. Who approved the ThirdParty Management scope?
<--- Score

61. Has everyone on the team, including the team leaders, been properly trained?
<--- Score

62. What are the Roles and Responsibilities for each team member and its leadership? Where is this documented?
<--- Score

63. How will variation in the actual durations of each activity be dealt with to ensure that the expected ThirdParty Management results are met?
<--- Score

64. Will a ThirdParty Management production readiness review be required?
<--- Score

65. How is the team tracking and documenting its work?
<--- Score

66. Has a ThirdParty Management requirement not been met?
<--- Score

67. What are the compelling stakeholder reasons for embarking on ThirdParty Management?
<--- Score

68. When are meeting minutes sent out? Who is on the distribution list?

<--- Score

69. Has the direction changed at all during the course of ThirdParty Management? If so, when did it change and why?
<--- Score

70. Are accountability and ownership for ThirdParty Management clearly defined?
<--- Score

71. What sort of initial information to gather?
<--- Score

72. Who are the ThirdParty Management improvement team members, including Management Leads and Coaches?
<--- Score

73. Has anyone else (internal or external to the group) attempted to solve this problem or a similar one before? If so, what knowledge can be leveraged from these previous efforts?
<--- Score

74. What are (control) requirements for ThirdParty Management Information?
<--- Score

75. Is ThirdParty Management currently on schedule according to the plan?
<--- Score

76. What information do you gather?
<--- Score

77. Will team members regularly document their ThirdParty Management work?
<--- Score

78. How did the ThirdParty Management manager receive input to the development of a ThirdParty Management improvement plan and the estimated completion dates/times of each activity?
<--- Score

79. What information should you gather?
<--- Score

80. How will the ThirdParty Management team and the group measure complete success of ThirdParty Management?
<--- Score

81. What is out-of-scope initially?
<--- Score

82. How can the value of ThirdParty Management be defined?
<--- Score

83. Is the work to date meeting requirements?
<--- Score

84. What defines best in class?
<--- Score

85. Are the ThirdParty Management requirements testable?
<--- Score

86. Is ThirdParty Management linked to key

stakeholder goals and objectives?
<--- Score

87. Is the ThirdParty Management scope manageable?
<--- Score

88. Are all requirements met?
<--- Score

89. What system do you use for gathering ThirdParty Management information?
<--- Score

90. Does the scope remain the same?
<--- Score

91. What ThirdParty Management services do you require?
<--- Score

92. What is out of scope?
<--- Score

93. If substitutes have been appointed, have they been briefed on the ThirdParty Management goals and received regular communications as to the progress to date?
<--- Score

94. Is the scope of ThirdParty Management defined?
<--- Score

95. What baselines are required to be defined and managed?
<--- Score

96. Are task requirements clearly defined?

<--- Score

97. Is there a completed, verified, and validated high-level 'as is' (not 'should be' or 'could be') stakeholder process map?

<--- Score

98. Is it clearly defined in and to your organization what you do?

<--- Score

99. What are the rough order estimates on cost savings/opportunities that ThirdParty Management brings?

<--- Score

100. Is the team equipped with available and reliable resources?

<--- Score

101. What are the core elements of the ThirdParty Management business case?

<--- Score

102. Who defines (or who defined) the rules and roles?

<--- Score

103. Has the improvement team collected the 'voice of the customer' (obtained feedback – qualitative and quantitative)?

<--- Score

104. How are consistent ThirdParty Management definitions important?

<--- Score

105. Do you have organizational privacy requirements?
<--- Score

106. What specifically is the problem? Where does it occur? When does it occur? What is its extent?
<--- Score

107. Scope of sensitive information?
<--- Score

108. Is there a completed SIPOC representation, describing the Suppliers, Inputs, Process, Outputs, and Customers?
<--- Score

109. What critical content must be communicated – who, what, when, where, and how?
<--- Score

110. What knowledge or experience is required?
<--- Score

111. How do you build the right business case?
<--- Score

112. Is there a clear ThirdParty Management case definition?
<--- Score

113. What is a worst-case scenario for losses?
<--- Score

114. Has a high-level 'as is' process map been completed, verified and validated?

<--- Score

115. What are the record-keeping requirements of ThirdParty Management activities?
<--- Score

116. Has/have the customer(s) been identified?
<--- Score

117. How do you gather ThirdParty Management requirements?
<--- Score

118. Is scope creep really all bad news?
<--- Score

119. What are the ThirdParty Management tasks and definitions?
<--- Score

120. Is full participation by members in regularly held team meetings guaranteed?
<--- Score

121. The political context: who holds power?
<--- Score

122. Has a project plan, Gantt chart, or similar been developed/completed?
<--- Score

123. Is the ThirdParty Management scope complete and appropriately sized?
<--- Score

124. What are the ThirdParty Management use cases?

<--- Score

125. What is the scope of ThirdParty Management?
<--- Score

126. Are the ThirdParty Management requirements complete?
<--- Score

127. Has a team charter been developed and communicated?
<--- Score

128. How was the 'as is' process map developed, reviewed, verified and validated?
<--- Score

129. Is ThirdParty Management required?
<--- Score

130. How do you gather the stories?
<--- Score

131. Are audit criteria, scope, frequency and methods defined?
<--- Score

132. Are different versions of process maps needed to account for the different types of inputs?
<--- Score

133. What happens if ThirdParty Management's scope changes?
<--- Score

134. Are approval levels defined for contracts and

supplements to contracts?
<--- Score

135. How do you manage changes in ThirdParty
Management requirements?
<--- Score

Add up total points for this section:
_____ = Total points for this section

Divided by: _____ (number of
statements answered) = _____
Average score for this section

Transfer your score to the ThirdParty
Management Index at the beginning of
the Self-Assessment.

CRITERION #3: MEASURE:

INTENT: Gather the correct data. Measure the current performance and evolution of the situation.

In my belief, the answer to this question is clearly defined:

5 Strongly Agree

4 Agree

3 Neutral

2 Disagree

1 Strongly Disagree

1. What methods are feasible and acceptable to estimate the impact of reforms?
<--- Score

2. Are ThirdParty Management vulnerabilities categorized and prioritized?
<--- Score

3. **Are you aware of what could cause a problem?**

<--- Score

4. What are the ThirdParty Management investment costs?
<--- Score

5. What is measured? Why?
<--- Score

6. What causes investor action?
<--- Score

7. What are your operating costs?
<--- Score

8. Where can you go to verify the info?
<--- Score

9. What could cause you to change course?
<--- Score

10. How sensitive must the ThirdParty Management strategy be to cost?
<--- Score

11. What details are required of the ThirdParty Management cost structure?
<--- Score

12. Do you have an issue in getting priority?
<--- Score

13. At what cost?
<--- Score

14. Are there any easy-to-implement alternatives

to ThirdParty Management? Sometimes other solutions are available that do not require the cost implications of a full-blown project?
<--- Score

15. Where is the cost?
<--- Score

16. Have design-to-cost goals been established?
<--- Score

17. Will ThirdParty Management have an impact on current business continuity, disaster recovery processes and/or infrastructure?
<--- Score

18. How do you aggregate measures across priorities?
<--- Score

19. How are measurements made?
<--- Score

20. What does your operating model cost?
<--- Score

21. How can you reduce the costs of obtaining inputs?
<--- Score

22. Did you tackle the cause or the symptom?
<--- Score

23. How do you measure efficient delivery of ThirdParty Management services?
<--- Score

24. What would be a real cause for concern?

<--- Score

25. How will costs be allocated?
<--- Score

26. How do you verify performance?
<--- Score

27. What are your customers expectations and measures?
<--- Score

28. How do you verify and develop ideas and innovations?
<--- Score

29. What is an unallowable cost?
<--- Score

30. Are there competing ThirdParty Management priorities?
<--- Score

31. Where is it measured?
<--- Score

32. Is the solution cost-effective?
<--- Score

33. How is progress measured?
<--- Score

34. What are the operational costs after ThirdParty Management deployment?
<--- Score

35. What harm might be caused?
<--- Score

36. How do you measure variability?
<--- Score

37. What are the strategic priorities for this year?
<--- Score

38. What could cause delays in the schedule?
<--- Score

39. What is the cost of rework?
<--- Score

40. Do you have a flow diagram of what happens?
<--- Score

41. Are supply costs steady or fluctuating?
<--- Score

42. Do the benefits outweigh the costs?
<--- Score

43. Do you effectively measure and reward individual and team performance?
<--- Score

44. Are the measurements objective?
<--- Score

45. How can you reduce costs?
<--- Score

46. What is your decision requirements diagram?
<--- Score

47. What are the costs?

<--- Score

48. What is the cause of any ThirdParty Management gaps?

<--- Score

49. What can be used to verify compliance?

<--- Score

50. How can a ThirdParty Management test verify your ideas or assumptions?

<--- Score

51. Are there measurements based on task performance?

<--- Score

52. What does a Test Case verify?

<--- Score

53. What relevant entities could be measured?

<--- Score

54. What are the costs of delaying ThirdParty Management action?

<--- Score

55. How can you measure the performance?

<--- Score

56. What measurements are possible, practicable and meaningful?

<--- Score

57. What are your primary costs, revenues, assets?
<--- Score

58. Do you verify that corrective actions were taken?
<--- Score

59. What drives O&M cost?
<--- Score

60. What is the ThirdParty Management business impact?
<--- Score

61. Are missed ThirdParty Management opportunities costing your organization money?
<--- Score

62. What tests verify requirements?
<--- Score

63. How frequently do you verify your ThirdParty Management strategy?
<--- Score

64. How do you verify the authenticity of the data and information used?
<--- Score

65. Do you aggressively reward and promote the people who have the biggest impact on creating excellent ThirdParty Management services/products?
<--- Score

66. How do you verify if ThirdParty Management is built right?
<--- Score

67. What disadvantage does this cause for the user?
<--- Score

68. What does verifying compliance entail?
<--- Score

69. Among the ThirdParty Management product and service cost to be estimated, which is considered hardest to estimate?
<--- Score

70. How is the value delivered by ThirdParty Management being measured?
<--- Score

71. How frequently do you track ThirdParty Management measures?
<--- Score

72. Is it possible to estimate the impact of unanticipated complexity such as wrong or failed assumptions, feedback, etcetera on proposed reforms?
<--- Score

73. How do you verify ThirdParty Management completeness and accuracy?
<--- Score

74. What does losing customers cost your organization?
<--- Score

75. What is the total fixed cost?
<--- Score

76. Has a cost center been established?

<--- Score

77. Which ThirdParty Management impacts are significant?

<--- Score

78. Is the cost worth the ThirdParty Management effort ?

<--- Score

79. How do you measure success?

<--- Score

80. What happens If cost savings do not materialize?

<--- Score

81. What causes extra work or rework?

<--- Score

82. Have you included everything in your ThirdParty Management cost models?

<--- Score

83. Are you able to realize any cost savings?

<--- Score

84. How do you verify your resources?

<--- Score

85. When are costs are incurred?

<--- Score

86. How will effects be measured?

<--- Score

87. How do you prevent mis-estimating cost?
<--- Score

88. How will you measure success?
<--- Score

89. What do you measure and why?
<--- Score

90. Are you taking your company in the direction of better and revenue or cheaper and cost?
<--- Score

91. Which measures and indicators matter?
<--- Score

92. What are your key ThirdParty Management organizational performance measures, including key short and longer-term financial measures?
<--- Score

93. What potential environmental factors impact the ThirdParty Management effort?
<--- Score

94. Who pays the cost?
<--- Score

95. What causes mismanagement?
<--- Score

96. Who should receive measurement reports?
<--- Score

97. How do your measurements capture actionable

ThirdParty Management information for use in exceeding your customers expectations and securing your customers engagement?
<--- Score

98. When a disaster occurs, who gets priority?
<--- Score

99. What are the ThirdParty Management key cost drivers?
<--- Score

100. How will measures be used to manage and adapt?
<--- Score

101. How long to keep data and how to manage retention costs?
<--- Score

102. What are you verifying?
<--- Score

103. What is the total cost related to deploying ThirdParty Management, including any consulting or professional services?
<--- Score

104. Which costs should be taken into account?
<--- Score

105. How much does it cost?
<--- Score

106. What measurements are being captured?
<--- Score

107. What would it cost to replace your technology?
<--- Score

108. What is the root cause(s) of the problem?
<--- Score

109. What are the current costs of the ThirdParty
Management process?
<--- Score

**110. Are indirect costs charged to the ThirdParty
Management program?**
<--- Score

111. What are the uncertainties surrounding estimates
of impact?
<--- Score

112. Why do you expend time and effort to
implement measurement, for whom?
<--- Score

113. What is your ThirdParty Management quality cost
segregation study?
<--- Score

114. How will you measure your ThirdParty
Management effectiveness?
<--- Score

115. What are the types and number of measures to
use?
<--- Score

116. How can you manage cost down?

<--- Score

117. What causes innovation to fail or succeed in your organization?
<--- Score

118. Does a ThirdParty Management quantification method exist?
<--- Score

119. What are hidden ThirdParty Management quality costs?
<--- Score

120. How do you quantify and qualify impacts?
<--- Score

121. How do you verify and validate the ThirdParty Management data?
<--- Score

122. Do you have any cost ThirdParty Management limitation requirements?
<--- Score

123. How can you measure ThirdParty Management in a systematic way?
<--- Score

124. Does the ThirdParty Management task fit the client's priorities?
<--- Score

125. What are allowable costs?
<--- Score

126. What do people want to verify?
<--- Score

127. How do you control the overall costs of your work processes?
<--- Score

128. When should you bother with diagrams?
<--- Score

129. Does management have the right priorities among projects?
<--- Score

130. What evidence is there and what is measured?
<--- Score

131. Are actual costs in line with budgeted costs?
<--- Score

132. What are the costs of reform?
<--- Score

133. Are the units of measure consistent?
<--- Score

134. How is performance measured?
<--- Score

135. How will your organization measure success?
<--- Score

Add up total points for this section:
_ _ _ _ _ = Total points for this section

Divided by: _ _ _ _ _ _ (number of

statements answered) = _____
Average score for this section

Transfer your score to the ThirdParty
Management Index at the beginning of
the Self-Assessment.

CRITERION #4: ANALYZE:

INTENT: Analyze causes, assumptions and hypotheses.

In my belief, the answer to this question is clearly defined:

5 Strongly Agree

4 Agree

3 Neutral

2 Disagree

1 Strongly Disagree

1. How do your work systems and key work processes relate to and capitalize on your core competencies?
<--- Score

2. How many input/output points does it require?
<--- Score

3. What do you need to qualify?
<--- Score

4. Are ThirdParty Management changes recognized early enough to be approved through the regular process?
<--- Score

5. What conclusions were drawn from the team's data collection and analysis? How did the team reach these conclusions?
<--- Score

6. Is the required ThirdParty Management data gathered?
<--- Score

7. Do your contracts/agreements contain data security obligations?
<--- Score

8. Were there any improvement opportunities identified from the process analysis?
<--- Score

9. Is pre-qualification of suppliers carried out?
<--- Score

10. Is there an established change management process?
<--- Score

11. Do staff qualifications match your project?
<--- Score

12. What systems/processes must you excel at?
<--- Score

13. What were the crucial 'moments of truth' on the

process map?

<--- Score

14. Who is involved in the management review process?

<--- Score

15. How will the change process be managed?

<--- Score

16. What is the output?

<--- Score

17. What qualifies as competition?

<--- Score

18. Has an output goal been set?

<--- Score

19. How do you promote understanding that opportunity for improvement is not criticism of the status quo, or the people who created the status quo?

<--- Score

20. Do you, as a leader, bounce back quickly from setbacks?

<--- Score

21. How do you identify specific ThirdParty Management investment opportunities and emerging trends?

<--- Score

22. What types of data do your ThirdParty Management indicators require?

<--- Score

23. Which ThirdParty Management data should be retained?

<--- Score

24. Do your employees have the opportunity to do what they do best everyday?

<--- Score

25. Is the suppliers process defined and controlled?

<--- Score

26. What is the cost of poor quality as supported by the team's analysis?

<--- Score

27. What output to create?

<--- Score

28. What are the personnel training and qualifications required?

<--- Score

29. Do several people in different organizational units assist with the ThirdParty Management process?

<--- Score

30. How difficult is it to qualify what ThirdParty Management ROI is?

<--- Score

31. Can you add value to the current ThirdParty Management decision-making process (largely qualitative) by incorporating uncertainty modeling (more quantitative)?

<--- Score

32. Are all staff in core ThirdParty Management subjects Highly Qualified?

<--- Score

33. What other organizational variables, such as reward systems or communication systems, affect the performance of this ThirdParty Management process?

<--- Score

34. Was a cause-and-effect diagram used to explore the different types of causes (or sources of variation)?

<--- Score

35. How is the data gathered?

<--- Score

36. Who owns what data?

<--- Score

37. When should a process be art not science?

<--- Score

38. How do you use ThirdParty Management data and information to support organizational decision making and innovation?

<--- Score

39. What methods do you use to gather ThirdParty Management data?

<--- Score

40. Should you invest in industry-recognized qualifications?

<--- Score

41. Think about some of the processes you undertake within your organization, which do you own?
<--- Score

42. How are outputs preserved and protected?
<--- Score

43. How will corresponding data be collected?
<--- Score

44. What qualifications do ThirdParty Management leaders need?
<--- Score

45. What other jobs or tasks affect the performance of the steps in the ThirdParty Management process?
<--- Score

46. Do you have the authority to produce the output?
<--- Score

47. Is the gap/opportunity displayed and communicated in financial terms?
<--- Score

48. What are the necessary qualifications?
<--- Score

49. What are the best opportunities for value improvement?
<--- Score

50. Who will gather what data?

<--- Score

51. What is your organizations system for selecting qualified vendors?
<--- Score

52. Have the problem and goal statements been updated to reflect the additional knowledge gained from the analyze phase?
<--- Score

53. Have any additional benefits been identified that will result from closing all or most of the gaps?
<--- Score

54. Are your outputs consistent?
<--- Score

55. Record-keeping requirements flow from the records needed as inputs, outputs, controls and for transformation of a ThirdParty Management process, are the records needed as inputs to the ThirdParty Management process available?
<--- Score

56. What training and qualifications will you need?
<--- Score

57. Do quality systems drive continuous improvement?
<--- Score

58. How is data used for program management and improvement?
<--- Score

59. How has the ThirdParty Management data been gathered?
<--- Score

60. Think about the functions involved in your ThirdParty Management project, what processes flow from these functions?
<--- Score

61. What controls do you have in place to protect data?
<--- Score

62. What is the ThirdParty Management Driver?
<--- Score

63. What ThirdParty Management data do you gather or use now?
<--- Score

64. What are the revised rough estimates of the financial savings/opportunity for ThirdParty Management improvements?
<--- Score

65. What are the ThirdParty Management business drivers?
<--- Score

66. What is the Value Stream Mapping?
<--- Score

67. How do you define collaboration and team output?
<--- Score

68. What process improvements will be needed?
<--- Score

69. What information qualified as important?
<--- Score

70. Where can you get qualified talent today?
<--- Score

71. Where is the data coming from to measure compliance?
<--- Score

72. Are you missing ThirdParty Management opportunities?
<--- Score

73. What ThirdParty Management data should be managed?
<--- Score

74. What is the complexity of the output produced?
<--- Score

75. How can risk management be tied procedurally to process elements?
<--- Score

76. How do you implement and manage your work processes to ensure that they meet design requirements?
<--- Score

77. Is the ThirdParty Management process severely broken such that a re-design is necessary?

<--- Score

78. What kind of crime could a potential new hire have committed that would not only not disqualify him/her from being hired by your organization, but would actually indicate that he/she might be a particularly good fit?
<--- Score

79. Was a detailed process map created to amplify critical steps of the 'as is' stakeholder process?
<--- Score

80. Is the performance gap determined?
<--- Score

81. How is ThirdParty Management data gathered?
<--- Score

82. What tools were used to generate the list of possible causes?
<--- Score

83. An organizationally feasible system request is one that considers the mission, goals and objectives of the organization, key questions are: is the ThirdParty Management solution request practical and will it solve a problem or take advantage of an opportunity to achieve company goals?
<--- Score

84. Have you defined which data is gathered how?
<--- Score

85. What ThirdParty Management data will be collected?

<--- Score

86. How often will data be collected for measures?
<--- Score

87. How will the ThirdParty Management data be captured?
<--- Score

88. What are your current levels and trends in key measures or indicators of ThirdParty Management product and process performance that are important to and directly serve your customers? How do these results compare with the performance of your competitors and other organizations with similar offerings?
<--- Score

89. What qualifications are needed?
<--- Score

90. Who gets your output?
<--- Score

91. What are your ThirdParty Management processes?
<--- Score

92. What ThirdParty Management data should be collected?
<--- Score

93. What are your best practices for minimizing ThirdParty Management project risk, while demonstrating incremental value and quick wins throughout the ThirdParty Management project lifecycle?

<--- Score

94. What, related to, ThirdParty Management processes does your organization outsource?
<--- Score

95. What does the data say about the performance of the stakeholder process?
<--- Score

96. How was the detailed process map generated, verified, and validated?
<--- Score

97. Is there any way to speed up the process?
<--- Score

98. How do you ensure that the ThirdParty Management opportunity is realistic?
<--- Score

99. Is data and process analysis, root cause analysis and quantifying the gap/opportunity in place?
<--- Score

100. How is the ThirdParty Management Value Stream Mapping managed?
<--- Score

101. Who is involved with workflow mapping?
<--- Score

102. What resources go in to get the desired output?
<--- Score

103. How does the organization define, manage,

and improve its ThirdParty Management processes?

<--- Score

104. Do your leaders quickly bounce back from setbacks?

<--- Score

105. How much data can be collected in the given timeframe?

<--- Score

106. What were the financial benefits resulting from any 'ground fruit or low-hanging fruit' (quick fixes)?

<--- Score

107. What qualifications and skills do you need?

<--- Score

108. What is the oversight process?

<--- Score

109. Is there a strict change management process?

<--- Score

110. A compounding model resolution with available relevant data can often provide insight towards a solution methodology; which ThirdParty Management models, tools and techniques are necessary?

<--- Score

111. Who qualifies to gain access to data?

<--- Score

112. How is the way you as the leader think and

process information affecting your organizational culture?

<--- Score

113. Were Pareto charts (or similar) used to portray the 'heavy hitters' (or key sources of variation)?

<--- Score

114. What process should you select for improvement?

<--- Score

115. What tools were used to narrow the list of possible causes?

<--- Score

116. What data do you need to collect?

<--- Score

117. What are evaluation criteria for the output?

<--- Score

118. Identify an operational issue in your organization, for example, could a particular task be done more quickly or more efficiently by ThirdParty Management?

<--- Score

119. Has data output been validated?

<--- Score

120. What are your outputs?

<--- Score

121. What will drive ThirdParty Management change?

<--- Score

122. Are all team members qualified for all tasks?
<--- Score

123. What quality tools were used to get through the analyze phase?
<--- Score

124. What is your organizations process which leads to recognition of value generation?
<--- Score

125. What internal processes need improvement?
<--- Score

126. Where is ThirdParty Management data gathered?
<--- Score

127. What ThirdParty Management metrics are outputs of the process?
<--- Score

128. Did any additional data need to be collected?
<--- Score

129. Were any designed experiments used to generate additional insight into the data analysis?
<--- Score

130. Did any value-added analysis or 'lean thinking' take place to identify some of the gaps shown on the 'as is' process map?
<--- Score

131. What data is gathered?

<--- Score

132. What did the team gain from developing a sub-process map?
<--- Score

133. What are your current levels and trends in key ThirdParty Management measures or indicators of product and process performance that are important to and directly serve your customers?
<--- Score

Add up total points for this section:
_ _ _ _ _ = Total points for this section

Divided by: _ _ _ _ _ _ (number of statements answered) = _ _ _ _ _ _
Average score for this section

Transfer your score to the ThirdParty Management Index at the beginning of the Self-Assessment.

CRITERION #5: IMPROVE:

INTENT: Develop a practical solution. Innovate, establish and test the solution and to measure the results.

In my belief, the answer to this question is clearly defined:

5 Strongly Agree

4 Agree

3 Neutral

2 Disagree

1 Strongly Disagree

1. What area needs the greatest improvement?
<--- Score

2. How does the team improve its work?
<--- Score

3. Have you identified breakpoints and/or risk tolerances that will trigger broad consideration of a potential need for intervention or modification of

strategy?

<--- Score

4. What do you want to improve?

<--- Score

5. Do you cover the five essential competencies: Communication, Collaboration,Innovation, Adaptability, and Leadership that improve an organizations ability to leverage the new ThirdParty Management in a volatile global economy?

<--- Score

6. How do you manage and improve your ThirdParty Management work systems to deliver customer value and achieve organizational success and sustainability?

<--- Score

7. What communications are necessary to support the implementation of the solution?

<--- Score

8. Who are the people involved in developing and implementing ThirdParty Management?

<--- Score

9. How do you improve your likelihood of success ?

<--- Score

10. Who manages supplier risk management in your organization?

<--- Score

11. How do you improve productivity?

<--- Score

12. What are your current levels and trends in key measures or indicators of workforce and leader development?
<--- Score

13. What are the ThirdParty Management security risks?
<--- Score

14. What is ThirdParty Management's impact on utilizing the best solution(s)?
<--- Score

15. Who controls the risk?
<--- Score

16. Are the key business and technology risks being managed?
<--- Score

17. What criteria will you use to assess your ThirdParty Management risks?
<--- Score

18. How are ThirdParty Management risks managed?
<--- Score

19. How do you deal with ThirdParty Management risk?
<--- Score

20. Is the ThirdParty Management solution sustainable?

<--- Score

21. How do you decide how much to remunerate an employee?
<--- Score

22. How can you better manage risk?
<--- Score

23. How do the ThirdParty Management results compare with the performance of your competitors and other organizations with similar offerings?
<--- Score

24. If you could go back in time five years, what decision would you make differently? What is your best guess as to what decision you're making today you might regret five years from now?
<--- Score

25. How do you manage ThirdParty Management risk?
<--- Score

26. At what point will vulnerability assessments be performed once ThirdParty Management is put into production (e.g., ongoing Risk Management after implementation)?
<--- Score

27. What lessons, if any, from a pilot were incorporated into the design of the full-scale solution?
<--- Score

28. What should a proof of concept or pilot accomplish?

<--- Score

29. Can you identify any significant risks or exposures to ThirdParty Management third- parties (vendors, service providers, alliance partners etc) that concern you?
<--- Score

30. What are the expected ThirdParty Management results?
<--- Score

31. What is the team's contingency plan for potential problems occurring in implementation?
<--- Score

32. Will the controls trigger any other risks?
<--- Score

33. Explorations of the frontiers of ThirdParty Management will help you build influence, improve ThirdParty Management, optimize decision making, and sustain change, what is your approach?
<--- Score

34. Have you achieved ThirdParty Management improvements?
<--- Score

35. What assumptions are made about the solution and approach?
<--- Score

36. What practices helps your organization to develop its capacity to recognize patterns?
<--- Score

37. How do you measure risk?
<--- Score

38. Are events managed to resolution?
<--- Score

39. How will you know that you have improved?
<--- Score

40. Is supporting ThirdParty Management documentation required?
<--- Score

41. For estimation problems, how do you develop an estimation statement?
<--- Score

42. What current systems have to be understood and/or changed?
<--- Score

43. What are the affordable ThirdParty Management risks?
<--- Score

44. Are the most efficient solutions problem-specific?
<--- Score

45. What are the implications of the one critical ThirdParty Management decision 10 minutes, 10 months, and 10 years from now?
<--- Score

46. How do you link measurement and risk?
<--- Score

47. To what extent does management recognize ThirdParty Management as a tool to increase the results?
<--- Score

48. What improvements have been achieved?
<--- Score

49. How do you measure progress and evaluate training effectiveness?
<--- Score

50. Who should make the ThirdParty Management decisions?
<--- Score

51. How scalable is your ThirdParty Management solution?
<--- Score

52. What is the magnitude of the improvements?
<--- Score

53. What attendant changes will need to be made to ensure that the solution is successful?
<--- Score

54. What were the underlying assumptions on the cost-benefit analysis?
<--- Score

55. How will you know when its improved?
<--- Score

56. Does a good decision guarantee a good outcome?

<--- Score

57. Was a ThirdParty Management charter developed?
<--- Score

58. How do you keep improving ThirdParty Management?
<--- Score

59. Is the scope clearly documented?
<--- Score

60. ThirdParty Management risk decisions: whose call Is It?
<--- Score

61. Are procedures documented for managing ThirdParty Management risks?
<--- Score

62. Can the solution be designed and implemented within an acceptable time period?
<--- Score

63. Is there a high likelihood that any recommendations will achieve their intended results?
<--- Score

64. What were the criteria for evaluating a ThirdParty Management pilot?
<--- Score

65. How do you go about comparing ThirdParty Management approaches/solutions?
<--- Score

66. Are decisions made in a timely manner?
<--- Score

67. For decision problems, how do you develop a decision statement?
<--- Score

68. What strategies for ThirdParty Management improvement are successful?
<--- Score

69. How do you improve ThirdParty Management service perception, and satisfaction?
<--- Score

70. What is the ThirdParty Management's sustainability risk?
<--- Score

71. Do you combine technical expertise with business knowledge and ThirdParty Management Key topics include lifecycles, development approaches, requirements and how to make a business case?
<--- Score

72. How risky is your organization?
<--- Score

73. What are the concrete ThirdParty Management results?
<--- Score

74. How will you measure the results?
<--- Score

75. What is the implementation plan?
<--- Score

76. When you map the key players in your own work and the types/domains of relationships with them, which relationships do you find easy and which challenging, and why?
<--- Score

77. Do vendor agreements bring new compliance risk ?
<--- Score

78. Is risk periodically assessed?
<--- Score

79. What tools do you use once you have decided on a ThirdParty Management strategy and more importantly how do you choose?
<--- Score

80. Who will be responsible for making the decisions to include or exclude requested changes once ThirdParty Management is underway?
<--- Score

81. How do you measure improved ThirdParty Management service perception, and satisfaction?
<--- Score

82. Who manages ThirdParty Management risk?
<--- Score

83. Who do you report ThirdParty Management results to?

<--- Score

84. How do you define the solutions' scope?
<--- Score

85. Who are the key stakeholders for the ThirdParty Management evaluation?
<--- Score

86. How will you know that a change is an improvement?
<--- Score

87. Who will be using the results of the measurement activities?
<--- Score

88. Risk factors: what are the characteristics of ThirdParty Management that make it risky?
<--- Score

89. Is any ThirdParty Management documentation required?
<--- Score

90. Risk Identification: What are the possible risk events your organization faces in relation to ThirdParty Management?
<--- Score

91. What error proofing will be done to address some of the discrepancies observed in the 'as is' process?
<--- Score

92. Where do you need ThirdParty Management improvement?

<--- Score

93. What does the 'should be' process map/design look like?
<--- Score

94. Are the risks fully understood, reasonable and manageable?
<--- Score

95. How are policy decisions made and where?
<--- Score

96. How can the phases of ThirdParty Management development be identified?
<--- Score

97. What actually has to improve and by how much?
<--- Score

98. Risk events: what are the things that could go wrong?
<--- Score

99. Are risk triggers captured?
<--- Score

100. Where do the ThirdParty Management decisions reside?
<--- Score

101. How do you mitigate ThirdParty Management risk?
<--- Score

102. What is the risk?
<--- Score

103. Is ThirdParty Management documentation maintained?
<--- Score

104. What ThirdParty Management improvements can be made?
<--- Score

105. What is ThirdParty Management risk?
<--- Score

106. Do those selected for the ThirdParty Management team have a good general understanding of what ThirdParty Management is all about?
<--- Score

107. What tools were most useful during the improve phase?
<--- Score

108. Are risk management tasks balanced centrally and locally?
<--- Score

109. How can skill-level changes improve ThirdParty Management?
<--- Score

110. How is continuous improvement applied to risk management?
<--- Score

111. How does your organization evaluate strategic ThirdParty Management success?
<--- Score

112. What tools were used to tap into the creativity and encourage 'outside the box' thinking?
<--- Score

113. Are you assessing ThirdParty Management and risk?
<--- Score

114. Who makes the ThirdParty Management decisions in your organization?
<--- Score

115. What can you do to improve?
<--- Score

116. Is the solution technically practical?
<--- Score

117. What resources are required for the improvement efforts?
<--- Score

118. How can you improve performance?
<--- Score

119. Is the ThirdParty Management documentation thorough?
<--- Score

120. How significant is the improvement in the eyes of the end user?
<--- Score

121. Who are the ThirdParty Management decision-makers?
<--- Score

122. What needs improvement? Why?
<--- Score

123. What went well, what should change, what can improve?
<--- Score

124. Which of the recognised risks out of all risks can be most likely transferred?
<--- Score

125. How will you recognize and celebrate results?
<--- Score

126. Does the goal represent a desired result that can be measured?
<--- Score

127. What tools were used to evaluate the potential solutions?
<--- Score

128. Who will be responsible for documenting the ThirdParty Management requirements in detail?
<--- Score

129. What to do with the results or outcomes of measurements?
<--- Score

130. Would you develop a ThirdParty Management

Communication Strategy?
<--- Score

131. How can you improve ThirdParty Management?
<--- Score

132. Who are the ThirdParty Management decision makers?
<--- Score

133. Do you have the optimal project management team structure?
<--- Score

134. What alternative responses are available to manage risk?
<--- Score

Add up total points for this section:
_ _ _ _ _ = Total points for this section

Divided by: _ _ _ _ _ _ (number of statements answered) = _ _ _ _ _ _
Average score for this section

Transfer your score to the ThirdParty Management Index at the beginning of the Self-Assessment.

CRITERION #6: CONTROL:

INTENT: Implement the practical solution. Maintain the performance and correct possible complications.

In my belief, the answer to this question is clearly defined:

5 Strongly Agree

4 Agree

3 Neutral

2 Disagree

1 Strongly Disagree

1. How do senior leaders actions reflect a commitment to the organizations ThirdParty Management values?
<--- Score

2. Is there documentation that will support the successful operation of the improvement?
<--- Score

3. Is knowledge gained on process shared and institutionalized?
<--- Score

4. Is there a recommended audit plan for routine surveillance inspections of ThirdParty Management's gains?
<--- Score

5. Do the viable solutions scale to future needs?
<--- Score

6. Does job training on the documented procedures need to be part of the process team's education and training?
<--- Score

7. Is there a ThirdParty Management Communication plan covering who needs to get what information when?
<--- Score

8. What is your plan to assess your security risks?
<--- Score

9. Will any special training be provided for results interpretation?
<--- Score

10. Has the ThirdParty Management value of standards been quantified?
<--- Score

11. Are pertinent alerts monitored, analyzed and distributed to appropriate personnel?
<--- Score

12. How widespread is its use?
<--- Score

13. Can support from partners be adjusted?
<--- Score

14. Is there a control plan in place for sustaining improvements (short and long-term)?
<--- Score

15. What can you control?
<--- Score

16. In the case of a ThirdParty Management project, the criteria for the audit derive from implementation objectives, an audit of a ThirdParty Management project involves assessing whether the recommendations outlined for implementation have been met, can you track that any ThirdParty Management project is implemented as planned, and is it working?
<--- Score

17. Are new process steps, standards, and documentation ingrained into normal operations?
<--- Score

18. How is ThirdParty Management project cost planned, managed, monitored?
<--- Score

19. Are controls in place and consistently applied?
<--- Score

20. What are you attempting to measure/monitor?

<--- Score

21. How do your controls stack up?
<--- Score

22. How will you measure your QA plan's effectiveness?
<--- Score

23. How will input, process, and output variables be checked to detect for sub-optimal conditions?
<--- Score

24. How do you encourage people to take control and responsibility?
<--- Score

25. Do you monitor the effectiveness of your ThirdParty Management activities?
<--- Score

26. What other areas of the group might benefit from the ThirdParty Management team's improvements, knowledge, and learning?
<--- Score

27. How do controls support value?
<--- Score

28. Is reporting being used or needed?
<--- Score

29. What are the key elements of your ThirdParty Management performance improvement system, including your evaluation, organizational learning, and innovation processes?

<--- Score

30. Are you measuring, monitoring and predicting ThirdParty Management activities to optimize operations and profitability, and enhancing outcomes?
<--- Score

31. Will existing staff require re-training, for example, to learn new business processes?
<--- Score

32. Does a troubleshooting guide exist or is it needed?
<--- Score

33. Are suggested corrective/restorative actions indicated on the response plan for known causes to problems that might surface?
<--- Score

34. Are documented procedures clear and easy to follow for the operators?
<--- Score

35. What are your results for key measures or indicators of the accomplishment of your ThirdParty Management strategy and action plans, including building and strengthening core competencies?
<--- Score

36. Have new or revised work instructions resulted?
<--- Score

37. How can you best use all of your knowledge repositories to enhance learning and sharing?

<--- Score

38. What do you stand for--and what are you against?
<--- Score

39. How is change control managed?
<--- Score

40. How will the day-to-day responsibilities for monitoring and continual improvement be transferred from the improvement team to the process owner?
<--- Score

41. Does the ThirdParty Management performance meet the customer's requirements?
<--- Score

42. Are there documented procedures?
<--- Score

43. Who controls critical resources?
<--- Score

44. Do the ThirdParty Management decisions you make today help people and the planet tomorrow?
<--- Score

45. Is the ThirdParty Management test/monitoring cost justified?
<--- Score

46. Will your goals reflect your program budget?
<--- Score

47. What should you measure to verify efficiency

gains?
<--- Score

48. What are the known security controls?
<--- Score

49. What are the critical parameters to watch?
<--- Score

50. How will the process owner verify improvement in present and future sigma levels, process capabilities?
<--- Score

51. What key inputs and outputs are being measured on an ongoing basis?
<--- Score

52. What are the performance and scale of the ThirdParty Management tools?
<--- Score

53. Implementation Planning: is a pilot needed to test the changes before a full roll out occurs?
<--- Score

54. How will new or emerging customer needs/requirements be checked/communicated to orient the process toward meeting the new specifications and continually reducing variation?
<--- Score

55. Are the planned controls working?
<--- Score

56. What is the control/monitoring plan?
<--- Score

57. What is the best design framework for ThirdParty Management organization now that, in a post industrial-age if the top-down, command and control model is no longer relevant?
<--- Score

58. Who sets the ThirdParty Management standards?
<--- Score

59. You may have created your quality measures at a time when you lacked resources, technology wasn't up to the required standard, or low service levels were the industry norm. Have those circumstances changed?
<--- Score

60. What ThirdParty Management standards are applicable?
<--- Score

61. Against what alternative is success being measured?
<--- Score

62. Is there a standardized process?
<--- Score

63. Act/Adjust: What Do you Need to Do Differently?
<--- Score

64. What are customers monitoring?
<--- Score

65. Who has control over resources?
<--- Score

66. Is a response plan in place for when the input, process, or output measures indicate an 'out-of-control' condition?
<--- Score

67. What is the recommended frequency of auditing?
<--- Score

68. Does ThirdParty Management appropriately measure and monitor risk?
<--- Score

69. How will report readings be checked to effectively monitor performance?
<--- Score

70. Is there an action plan in case of emergencies?
<--- Score

71. How might the group capture best practices and lessons learned so as to leverage improvements?
<--- Score

72. Has the improved process and its steps been standardized?
<--- Score

73. Will the team be available to assist members in planning investigations?
<--- Score

74. Who is going to spread your message?
<--- Score

75. How will ThirdParty Management decisions be

made and monitored?
<--- Score

76. How will the process owner and team be able to hold the gains?
<--- Score

77. How likely is the current ThirdParty Management plan to come in on schedule or on budget?
<--- Score

78. Is there a documented and implemented monitoring plan?
<--- Score

79. How do you select, collect, align, and integrate ThirdParty Management data and information for tracking daily operations and overall organizational performance, including progress relative to strategic objectives and action plans?
<--- Score

80. Are the ThirdParty Management standards challenging?
<--- Score

81. Who is the ThirdParty Management process owner?
<--- Score

82. What do your reports reflect?
<--- Score

83. What do you measure to verify effectiveness gains?
<--- Score

84. Is a response plan established and deployed?
<--- Score

85. Does the response plan contain a definite closed loop continual improvement scheme (e.g., plan-do-check-act)?
<--- Score

86. Is there a transfer of ownership and knowledge to process owner and process team tasked with the responsibilities.
<--- Score

87. What other systems, operations, processes, and infrastructures (hiring practices, staffing, training, incentives/rewards, metrics/dashboards/scorecards, etc.) need updates, additions, changes, or deletions in order to facilitate knowledge transfer and improvements?
<--- Score

88. What quality tools were useful in the control phase?
<--- Score

89. What adjustments to the strategies are needed?
<--- Score

90. Can you adapt and adjust to changing ThirdParty Management situations?
<--- Score

91. How do you establish and deploy modified action plans if circumstances require a shift in plans and rapid execution of new plans?

<--- Score

92. How do you monitor usage and cost?
<--- Score

93. What should the next improvement project be that is related to ThirdParty Management?
<--- Score

94. How do you plan on providing proper recognition and disclosure of supporting companies?
<--- Score

95. Where do ideas that reach policy makers and planners as proposals for ThirdParty Management strengthening and reform actually originate?
<--- Score

96. Are the planned controls in place?
<--- Score

97. Are operating procedures consistent?
<--- Score

98. What is the standard for acceptable ThirdParty Management performance?
<--- Score

99. Do you monitor the ThirdParty Management decisions made and fine tune them as they evolve?
<--- Score

100. Is new knowledge gained imbedded in the response plan?
<--- Score

101. How do you spread information?
<--- Score

Add up total points for this section:
_ _ _ _ _ = Total points for this section

Divided by: _ _ _ _ _ _ (number of
statements answered) = _ _ _ _ _ _
Average score for this section

Transfer your score to the ThirdParty
Management Index at the beginning of
the Self-Assessment.

CRITERION #7: SUSTAIN:

INTENT: Retain the benefits.

In my belief, the answer to this question is clearly defined:

5 Strongly Agree

4 Agree

3 Neutral

2 Disagree

1 Strongly Disagree

1. What is your BATNA (best alternative to a negotiated agreement)?
<--- Score

2. What are the potential basics of ThirdParty Management fraud?
<--- Score

3. Do you have past ThirdParty Management successes?
<--- Score

4. Do you have enough freaky customers in your portfolio pushing you to the limit day in and day out?
<--- Score

5. Are you / should you be revolutionary or evolutionary?
<--- Score

6. What may be the consequences for the performance of an organization if all stakeholders are not consulted regarding ThirdParty Management?
<--- Score

7. Who are your customers?
<--- Score

8. What is effective ThirdParty Management?
<--- Score

9. What happens when a new employee joins the organization?
<--- Score

10. What is the big ThirdParty Management idea?
<--- Score

11. What is the craziest thing you can do?
<--- Score

12. What are the top 3 things at the forefront of your ThirdParty Management agendas for the next 3 years?
<--- Score

13. How do you deal with ThirdParty Management

changes?
<--- Score

14. Do ThirdParty Management rules make a reasonable demand on a users capabilities?
<--- Score

15. What role does communication play in the success or failure of a ThirdParty Management project?
<--- Score

16. What is the source of the strategies for ThirdParty Management strengthening and reform?
<--- Score

17. What is it like to work for you?
<--- Score

18. Who is responsible for ThirdParty Management?
<--- Score

19. Is a ThirdParty Management team work effort in place?
<--- Score

20. What ThirdParty Management skills are most important?
<--- Score

21. What happens at your organization when people fail?
<--- Score

22. How likely is it that a customer would recommend

your company to a friend or colleague?
<--- Score

23. How do you keep records, of what?
<--- Score

24. What will be the consequences to the stakeholder (financial, reputation etc) if ThirdParty Management does not go ahead or fails to deliver the objectives?
<--- Score

25. Who are four people whose careers you have enhanced?
<--- Score

26. Have benefits been optimized with all key stakeholders?
<--- Score

27. What is the recommended frequency of auditing?
<--- Score

28. Is it economical; do you have the time and money?
<--- Score

29. Who is on the team?
<--- Score

30. Think of your ThirdParty Management project, what are the main functions?
<--- Score

31. How much contingency will be available in the budget?
<--- Score

32. How will you know that the ThirdParty
Management project has been successful?
<--- Score

33. How do you go about securing ThirdParty
Management?
<--- Score

34. What you are going to do to affect the numbers?
<--- Score

35. Did your employees make progress today?
<--- Score

**36. Do you feel that more should be done in the
ThirdParty Management area?**
<--- Score

37. What are specific ThirdParty Management rules to
follow?
<--- Score

38. Who do we want your customers to become?
<--- Score

39. What is something you believe that nearly no one
agrees with you on?
<--- Score

40. What are strategies for increasing support and
reducing opposition?
<--- Score

41. How do you manage ThirdParty Management
Knowledge Management (KM)?
<--- Score

42. How do you make it meaningful in connecting ThirdParty Management with what users do day-to-day?
<--- Score

43. To whom do you add value?
<--- Score

44. Are assumptions made in ThirdParty Management stated explicitly?
<--- Score

45. How do you maintain ThirdParty Management's Integrity?
<--- Score

46. What trouble can you get into?
<--- Score

47. Is there any existing ThirdParty Management governance structure?
<--- Score

48. How do you assess the ThirdParty Management pitfalls that are inherent in implementing it?
<--- Score

49. How can you negotiate ThirdParty Management successfully with a stubborn boss, an irate client, or a deceitful coworker?
<--- Score

50. Who do you want your customers to become?
<--- Score

51. Who will determine interim and final deadlines?
<--- Score

52. Who is responsible for ensuring appropriate resources (time, people and money) are allocated to ThirdParty Management?
<--- Score

53. Which ThirdParty Management goals are the most important?
<--- Score

54. What must you excel at?
<--- Score

55. Are your responses positive or negative?
<--- Score

56. How do senior leaders deploy your organizations vision and values through your leadership system, to the workforce, to key suppliers and partners, and to customers and other stakeholders, as appropriate?
<--- Score

57. What are the rules and assumptions your industry operates under? What if the opposite were true?
<--- Score

58. What business benefits will ThirdParty Management goals deliver if achieved?
<--- Score

59. Ask yourself: how would you do this work if you only had one staff member to do it?
<--- Score

60. If there were zero limitations, what would you do differently?
<--- Score

61. How do you engage the workforce, in addition to satisfying them?
<--- Score

62. What would you recommend your friend do if he/she were facing this dilemma?
<--- Score

63. Are the assumptions believable and achievable?
<--- Score

64. How do you provide a safe environment -physically and emotionally?
<--- Score

65. When information truly is ubiquitous, when reach and connectivity are completely global, when computing resources are infinite, and when a whole new set of impossibilities are not only possible, but happening, what will that do to your business?
<--- Score

66. How can you become more high-tech but still be high touch?
<--- Score

67. What do we do when new problems arise?
<--- Score

68. What are you challenging?
<--- Score

69. Who uses your product in ways you never expected?
<--- Score

70. What are the essentials of internal ThirdParty Management management?
<--- Score

71. Do you see more potential in people than they do in themselves?
<--- Score

72. What is the overall talent health of your organization as a whole at senior levels, and for each organization reporting to a member of the Senior Leadership Team?
<--- Score

73. Do you have the right capabilities and capacities?
<--- Score

74. If you do not follow, then how to lead?
<--- Score

75. What is the range of capabilities?
<--- Score

76. How do you lead with ThirdParty Management in mind?
<--- Score

77. How do customers see your organization?
<--- Score

78. Are you using a design thinking approach and integrating Innovation, ThirdParty Management

Experience, and Brand Value?

<--- Score

79. Do you have an implicit bias for capital investments over people investments?

<--- Score

80. What are the key enablers to make this ThirdParty Management move?

<--- Score

81. Which individuals, teams or departments will be involved in ThirdParty Management?

<--- Score

82. Who is responsible for errors?

<--- Score

83. Why is ThirdParty Management important for you now?

<--- Score

84. What are the short and long-term ThirdParty Management goals?

<--- Score

85. If your company went out of business tomorrow, would anyone who doesn't get a paycheck here care?

<--- Score

86. How do you know if you are successful?

<--- Score

87. Do you know who is a friend or a foe?

<--- Score

88. What is the overall business strategy?
<--- Score

89. Are you relevant? Will you be relevant five years from now? Ten?
<--- Score

90. Is there any reason to believe the opposite of my current belief?
<--- Score

91. What is your formula for success in ThirdParty Management ?
<--- Score

92. How will you motivate the stakeholders with the least vested interest?
<--- Score

93. What projects are going on in the organization today, and what resources are those projects using from the resource pools?
<--- Score

94. How can you become the company that would put you out of business?
<--- Score

95. Who, on the executive team or the board, has spoken to a customer recently?
<--- Score

96. Which models, tools and techniques are necessary?
<--- Score

97. What are current ThirdParty Management paradigms?
<--- Score

98. What are the long-term ThirdParty Management goals?
<--- Score

99. How do you proactively clarify deliverables and ThirdParty Management quality expectations?
<--- Score

100. What counts that you are not counting?
<--- Score

101. Why should people listen to you?
<--- Score

102. Who are the key stakeholders?
<--- Score

103. How long will it take to change?
<--- Score

104. If your customer were your grandmother, would you tell her to buy what you're selling?
<--- Score

105. What goals did you miss?
<--- Score

106. Can you do all this work?
<--- Score

107. Who will be responsible for deciding whether ThirdParty Management goes ahead or not after the

initial investigations?
<--- Score

108. Can you break it down?
<--- Score

109. Do you say no to customers for no reason?
<--- Score

110. What happens if you do not have enough funding?
<--- Score

111. Whom among your colleagues do you trust, and for what?
< Score

112. What are the usability implications of ThirdParty Management actions?
<--- Score

113. What are your most important goals for the strategic ThirdParty Management objectives?
<--- Score

114. What is your ThirdParty Management strategy?
<--- Score

115. What have you done to protect your business from competitive encroachment?
<--- Score

116. Who else should you help?
<--- Score

117. How do you set ThirdParty Management stretch

targets and how do you get people to not only participate in setting these stretch targets but also that they strive to achieve these?
<--- Score

118. In retrospect, of the projects that you pulled the plug on, what percent do you wish had been allowed to keep going, and what percent do you wish had ended earlier?
<--- Score

119. Who will manage the integration of tools?
<--- Score

120. Instead of going to current contacts for new ideas, what if you reconnected with dormant contacts--the people you used to know? If you were going reactivate a dormant tie, who would it be?
<--- Score

121. Has implementation been effective in reaching specified objectives so far?
<--- Score

122. In the past year, what have you done (or could you have done) to increase the accurate perception of your company/brand as ethical and honest?
<--- Score

123. What are the gaps in your knowledge and experience?
<--- Score

124. How do you stay inspired?
<--- Score

125. Is your basic point _____ or _____?
<--- Score

126. How do you foster the skills, knowledge, talents, attributes, and characteristics you want to have?
<--- Score

127. How does ThirdParty Management integrate with other stakeholder initiatives?
<--- Score

128. If you got fired and a new hire took your place, what would she do different?
<--- Score

129. How much does ThirdParty Management help?
<--- Score

130. Why should you adopt a ThirdParty Management framework?
<--- Score

131. What potential megatrends could make your business model obsolete?
<--- Score

132. Do you think ThirdParty Management accomplishes the goals you expect it to accomplish?
<--- Score

133. Why is it important to have senior management support for a ThirdParty Management project?
<--- Score

134. Can the schedule be done in the given time?

<--- Score

135. Is the ThirdParty Management organization completing tasks effectively and efficiently?
<--- Score

136. Whose voice (department, ethnic group, women, older workers, etc) might you have missed hearing from in your company, and how might you amplify this voice to create positive momentum for your business?
<--- Score

137. What is an unauthorized commitment?
<--- Score

138. If you had to leave your organization for a year and the only communication you could have with employees/colleagues was a single paragraph, what would you write?
<--- Score

139. Is the impact that ThirdParty Management has shown?
<--- Score

140. Operational - will it work?
<--- Score

141. Will it be accepted by users?
<--- Score

142. Can you maintain your growth without detracting from the factors that have contributed to your success?
<--- Score

143. What management system can you use to leverage the ThirdParty Management experience, ideas, and concerns of the people closest to the work to be done?
<--- Score

144. What have been your experiences in defining long range ThirdParty Management goals?
<--- Score

145. How can you incorporate support to ensure safe and effective use of ThirdParty Management into the services that you provide?
<--- Score

146. What new services of functionality will be implemented next with ThirdParty Management ?
<--- Score

147. Why will customers want to buy your organizations products/services?
<--- Score

148. How do you listen to customers to obtain actionable information?
<--- Score

149. How do you create buy-in?
<--- Score

150. Would you rather sell to knowledgeable and informed customers or to uninformed customers?
<--- Score

151. How will you insure seamless interoperability

of ThirdParty Management moving forward?
<--- Score

152. What did you miss in the interview for the worst hire you ever made?
<--- Score

153. How do you track customer value, profitability or financial return, organizational success, and sustainability?
<--- Score

154. Marketing budgets are tighter, consumers are more skeptical, and social media has changed forever the way we talk about ThirdParty Management, how do you gain traction?
<--- Score

155. What is your competitive advantage?
<--- Score

156. Are new benefits received and understood?
<--- Score

157. Are you paying enough attention to the partners your company depends on to succeed?
<--- Score

158. Is a ThirdParty Management breakthrough on the horizon?
<--- Score

159. What should you stop doing?
<--- Score

160. Is maximizing ThirdParty Management

protection the same as minimizing ThirdParty Management loss?

<--- Score

161. How do you keep the momentum going?

<--- Score

162. Which functions and people interact with the supplier and or customer?

<--- Score

163. If you find that you havent accomplished one of the goals for one of the steps of the ThirdParty Management strategy, what will you do to fix it?

<--- Score

164. Do you have the right people on the bus?

<--- Score

165. Political -is anyone trying to undermine this project?

<--- Score

166. What are you trying to prove to yourself, and how might it be hijacking your life and business success?

<--- Score

167. Are there any activities that you can take off your to do list?

<--- Score

168. Are you maintaining a past–present–future perspective throughout the ThirdParty Management discussion?

<--- Score

169. How do you accomplish your long range ThirdParty Management goals?

<--- Score

170. How do you ensure that implementations of ThirdParty Management products are done in a way that ensures safety?

<--- Score

171. How do you transition from the baseline to the target?

<--- Score

172. Who have you, as a company, historically been when you've been at your best?

<--- Score

173. Is ThirdParty Management dependent on the successful delivery of a current project?

<--- Score

174. Who is the main stakeholder, with ultimate responsibility for driving ThirdParty Management forward?

<--- Score

175. How do you govern and fulfill your societal responsibilities?

<--- Score

176. Will there be any necessary staff changes (redundancies or new hires)?

<--- Score

177. What trophy do you want on your mantle?

<--- Score

178. If no one would ever find out about your accomplishments, how would you lead differently?
<--- Score

179. What is the estimated value of the project?
<--- Score

180. What are the success criteria that will indicate that ThirdParty Management objectives have been met and the benefits delivered?
<--- Score

181. Were lessons learned captured and communicated?
<--- Score

182. Who will provide the final approval of ThirdParty Management deliverables?
<--- Score

183. How is implementation research currently incorporated into each of your goals?
<--- Score

184. If you weren't already in this business, would you enter it today? And if not, what are you going to do about it?
<--- Score

185. Have new benefits been realized?
<--- Score

186. Are the criteria for selecting recommendations stated?

<--- Score

187. If you had to rebuild your organization without any traditional competitive advantages (i.e., no killer technology, promising research, innovative product/service delivery model, etcetera), how would your people have to approach their work and collaborate together in order to create the necessary conditions for success?
<--- Score

188. What are internal and external ThirdParty Management relations?
<--- Score

189. Are you making progress, and are you making progress as ThirdParty Management leaders?
<--- Score

190. What is the kind of project structure that would be appropriate for your ThirdParty Management project, should it be formal and complex, or can it be less formal and relatively simple?
<--- Score

191. Are you satisfied with your current role? If not, what is missing from it?
<--- Score

192. In a project to restructure ThirdParty Management outcomes, which stakeholders would you involve?
<--- Score

193. What are your personal philosophies regarding ThirdParty Management and how do they influence

your work?
<--- Score

194. What one word do you want to own in the minds of your customers, employees, and partners?
<--- Score

195. Are all key stakeholders present at all Structured Walkthroughs?
<--- Score

196. What is the purpose of ThirdParty Management in relation to the mission?
<--- Score

197. If you were responsible for initiating and implementing major changes in your organization, what steps might you take to ensure acceptance of those changes?
<--- Score

198. What would have to be true for the option on the table to be the best possible choice?
<--- Score

199. How will you ensure you get what you expected?
<--- Score

200. How are you doing compared to your industry?
<--- Score

201. What relationships among ThirdParty Management trends do you perceive?
<--- Score

202. What threat is ThirdParty Management addressing?
<--- Score

203. How do you foster innovation?
<--- Score

204. What is the funding source for this project?
<--- Score

205. What information is critical to your organization that your executives are ignoring?
<--- Score

206. How important is ThirdParty Management to the user organizations mission?
<--- Score

207. How do you determine the key elements that affect ThirdParty Management workforce satisfaction, how are these elements determined for different workforce groups and segments?
<--- Score

208. Is there a work around that you can use?
<--- Score

209. What is a feasible sequencing of reform initiatives over time?
<--- Score

210. What was the last experiment you ran?
<--- Score

211. Why not do ThirdParty Management?
<--- Score

212. Do you know what you are doing? And who do you call if you don't?
<--- Score

213. What stupid rule would you most like to kill?
<--- Score

214. What is your question? Why?
<--- Score

215. What ThirdParty Management modifications can you make work for you?
<--- Score

216. Who do you think the world wants your organization to be?
<--- Score

217. What are the challenges?
<--- Score

218. Is ThirdParty Management realistic, or are you setting yourself up for failure?
<--- Score

219. How do you cross-sell and up-sell your ThirdParty Management success?
<--- Score

Add up total points for this section:
_ _ _ _ _ = Total points for this section

Divided by: _ _ _ _ _ _ (number of statements answered) = _ _ _ _ _ _
Average score for this section

Transfer your score to the ThirdParty
Management Index at the beginning of
the Self-Assessment.

ThirdParty Management and Managing Projects, Criteria for Project Managers:

1.0 Initiating Process Group: ThirdParty Management

1. For technology ThirdParty Management projects only: Are all production support stakeholders (Business unit, technical support, & user) prepared for implementation with appropriate contingency plans?

2. Were resources available as planned?

3. Are you properly tracking the progress of the ThirdParty Management project and communicating the status to stakeholders?

4. Who is involved in each phase?

5. How to control and approve each phase?

6. What areas does the group agree are the biggest success on the ThirdParty Management project?

7. Were escalated issues resolved promptly?

8. Professionals want to know what is expected from them what are the deliverables?

9. Mitigate. what will you do to minimize the impact should the risk event occur?

10. Have requirements been tested, approved, and fulfill the ThirdParty Management project scope?

11. During which stage of Risk planning are risks prioritized based on probability and impact?

12. Specific - is the objective clear in terms of what, how, when, and where the situation will be changed?

13. How is each deliverable reviewed, verified, and validated?

14. Which six sigma dmaic phase focuses on why and how defects and errors occur?

15. Will the ThirdParty Management project meet the client requirements, and will it achieve the business success criteria that justified doing the ThirdParty Management project in the first place?

16. When are the deliverables to be generated in each phase?

17. Who is funding the ThirdParty Management project?

18. Are the changes in your ThirdParty Management project being formally requested, analyzed, and approved by the appropriate decision makers?

19. How can you make your needs known?

20. Do you know if the ThirdParty Management project requires outside equipment or vendor resources?

1.1 Project Charter: ThirdParty Management

21. Major high-level milestone targets: what events measure progress?

22. What is in it for you?

23. Customer: who are you doing the ThirdParty Management project for?

24. What goes into your ThirdParty Management project Charter?

25. Is time of the essence?

26. What does it need to do?

27. Assumptions and constraints: what assumptions were made in defining the ThirdParty Management project?

28. Why is a ThirdParty Management project Charter used?

29. Customer benefits: what customer requirements does this ThirdParty Management project address?

30. When?

31. How are ThirdParty Management projects different from operations?

32. How will you know that a change is an improvement?

33. Why the improvements?

34. What changes can you make to improve?

35. Success determination factors: how will the success of the ThirdParty Management project be determined from the customers perspective?

36. What outcome, in measureable terms, are you hoping to accomplish?

37. Name and describe the elements that deal with providing the detail?

38. What are some examples of a business case?

39. Run it as as a startup?

40. How do you manage integration?

1.2 Stakeholder Register: ThirdParty Management

41. How big is the gap?

42. Who wants to talk about Security?

43. What are the major ThirdParty Management project milestones requiring communications or providing communications opportunities?

44. What is the power of the stakeholder?

45. What & Why?

46. How should employers make voices heard?

47. Who is managing stakeholder engagement?

48. Is your organization ready for change?

49. What opportunities exist to provide communications?

50. How will reports be created?

51. Who are the stakeholders?

52. How much influence do they have on the ThirdParty Management project?

1.3 Stakeholder Analysis Matrix: ThirdParty Management

53. Where are the good opportunities facing your organizations development?

54. What are the mechanisms of public and social accountability, and how can they be made better?

55. Are they likely to influence the success or failure of your ThirdParty Management project?

56. Sustaining internal capabilities?

57. How can you counter negative efforts?

58. What are the opportunities for communication?

59. Technology development and innovation?

60. Guiding question: what is the issue at stake?

61. Who is influential in the ThirdParty Management project area (both thematic and geographic areas)?

62. What mechanisms are proposed to monitor and measure ThirdParty Management project performance in terms of social development outcomes?

63. Why do you care?

64. Usps (unique selling points)?

65. Who influences whom?

66. Who will promote/support the ThirdParty Management project, provided that they are involved?

67. Who determines value?

68. New markets, vertical, horizontal?

69. How will the stakeholder directly benefit from the ThirdParty Management project and how will this affect the stakeholders motivation?

70. Opponents; who are the opponents?

71. What advantages do your organizations stakeholders have?

72. Who will be responsible for managing the outcome?

2.0 Planning Process Group: ThirdParty Management

73. Are there efficient coordination mechanisms to avoid overloading the counterparts, participating stakeholders?

74. How well defined and documented are the ThirdParty Management project management processes you chose to use?

75. What makes your ThirdParty Management project successful?

76. Are work methodologies, financial instruments, etc. shared among departments, organizations and ThirdParty Management projects?

77. How can you tell when you are done?

78. To what extent is the program helping to influence your organizations policy framework?

79. To what extent have public/private national resources and/or counterparts been mobilized to contribute to the programs objective and produce results and impacts?

80. Product breakdown structure (pbs): what is the ThirdParty Management project result or product, and how should it look like, what are its parts?

81. Just how important is your work to the overall

success of the ThirdParty Management project?

82. What factors are contributing to progress or delay in the achievement of products and results?

83. Will you be replaced?

84. Why do it ThirdParty Management projects fail?

85. Is the ThirdParty Management project making progress in helping to achieve the set results?

86. Have more efficient (sensitive) and appropriate measures been adopted to respond to the political and socio-cultural problems identified?

87. Is the identification of the problems, inequalities and gaps, with respective causes, clear in the ThirdParty Management project?

88. When will the ThirdParty Management project be done?

89. What will you do?

90. If action is called for, what form should it take?

91. The ThirdParty Management project charter is created in which ThirdParty Management project management process group?

2.1 Project Management Plan: ThirdParty Management

92. Are cost risk analysis methods applied to develop contingencies for the estimated total ThirdParty Management project costs?

93. When is a ThirdParty Management project management plan created?

94. What went wrong?

95. Are there any Client staffing expectations?

96. Why Change?

97. What are the known stakeholder requirements?

98. Is the budget realistic?

99. Are the proposed ThirdParty Management project purposes different than a previously authorized ThirdParty Management project?

100. Are there any scope changes proposed for a previously authorized ThirdParty Management project?

101. Are alternatives safe, functional, constructible, economical, reasonable and sustainable?

102. What is risk management?

103. What are the assumptions?

104. What happened during the process that you found interesting?

105. What are the training needs?

106. How do you organize the costs in the ThirdParty Management project management plan?

107. Is there anything you would now do differently on your ThirdParty Management project based on past experience?

108. Will you add a schedule and diagram?

109. Who manages integration?

110. Are calculations and results of analyzes essentially correct?

111. If the ThirdParty Management project management plan is a comprehensive document that guides you in ThirdParty Management project execution and control, then what should it NOT contain?

2.2 Scope Management Plan: ThirdParty Management

112. How do you plan to control Scope Creep?

113. Is your organization structure for both tracking & controlling the budget well defined and assigned to a specific individual?

114. Alignment to strategic goals & objectives?

115. Are metrics used to evaluate and manage Vendors?

116. What weaknesses do you have?

117. Is current scope of the ThirdParty Management project substantially different than that originally defined?

118. Are procurement deliverables arriving on time and to specification?

119. Are updated ThirdParty Management project time & resource estimates reasonable based on the current ThirdParty Management project stage?

120. Does the detailed work plan match the complexity of tasks with the capabilities of personnel?

121. Is it standard practice to formally commit stakeholders to the ThirdParty Management project via agreements?

122. Are vendor invoices audited for accuracy before payment?

123. Is the communication plan being followed?

124. Has stakeholder analysis been conducted, assessing influence on the ThirdParty Management project and authority levels?

125. What are the risks of not having good inter-organization cooperation on the ThirdParty Management project?

126. What if you do not have more detailed information on the report?

127. Cost / benefit analysis?

128. What threats might prevent you from getting there?

129. Is there an issues management plan in place?

130. Do you keep stake holders informed?

2.3 Requirements Management Plan: ThirdParty Management

131. Business analysis scope?

132. Are actual resource expenditures versus planned still acceptable?

133. Did you avoid subjective, flowery or non-specific statements?

134. How will the requirements become prioritized?

135. Is stakeholder risk tolerance an important factor for the requirements process in this ThirdParty Management project?

136. Who came up with this requirement?

137. Will you document changes to requirements?

138. What are you counting on?

139. Have stakeholders been instructed in the Change Control process?

140. Will the product release be stable and mature enough to be deployed in the user community?

141. How knowledgeable is the primary Stakeholder(s) in the proposed application area?

142. What performance metrics will be used?

143. Will you perform a Requirements Risk assessment and develop a plan to deal with risks?

144. Will the contractors involved take full responsibility?

145. Did you provide clear and concise specifications?

146. Is there formal agreement on who has authority to request a change in requirements?

147. Is there formal agreement on who has authority to approve a change in requirements?

148. What is a problem?

149. Is the system software (non-operating system) new to the IT ThirdParty Management project team?

150. How will the information be distributed?

2.4 Requirements Documentation: ThirdParty Management

151. If applicable; are there issues linked with the fact that this is an offshore ThirdParty Management project?

152. Can the requirements be checked?

153. Has requirements gathering uncovered information that would necessitate changes?

154. Does the system provide the functions which best support the customers needs?

155. How does the proposed ThirdParty Management project contribute to the overall objectives of your organization?

156. What kind of entity is a problem ?

157. Do your constraints stand?

158. What is your Elevator Speech?

159. Does your organization restrict technical alternatives?

160. Completeness. are all functions required by the customer included?

161. What facilities must be supported by the system?

162. What will be the integration problems?

163. Can you check system requirements?

164. How much does requirements engineering cost?

165. Who provides requirements?

166. What is a show stopper in the requirements?

167. How do you know when a Requirement is accurate enough?

168. How linear / iterative is your Requirements Gathering process (or will it be)?

169. What images does it conjure?

170. How can you document system requirements?

2.5 Requirements Traceability Matrix: ThirdParty Management

171. Why do you manage scope?

172. What is the WBS?

173. Is there a requirements traceability process in place?

174. What percentage of ThirdParty Management projects are producing traceability matrices between requirements and other work products?

175. What are the chronologies, contingencies, consequences, criteria?

176. Will you use a Requirements Traceability Matrix?

177. How will it affect the stakeholders personally in career?

178. Describe the process for approving requirements so they can be added to the traceability matrix and ThirdParty Management project work can be performed. Will the ThirdParty Management project requirements become approved in writing?

179. How do you manage scope?

180. How small is small enough?

181. Why use a WBS?

182. Do you have a clear understanding of all subcontracts in place?

2.6 Project Scope Statement: ThirdParty Management

183. What process would you recommend for creating the ThirdParty Management project scope statement?

184. If the scope changes, what will the impact be to your ThirdParty Management project in terms of duration, cost, quality, or any other important areas of the ThirdParty Management project?

185. Were key ThirdParty Management project stakeholders brought into the ThirdParty Management project Plan?

186. Will an issue form be in use?

187. Is the scope of your ThirdParty Management project well defined?

188. Relevant - ask yourself can you get there; why are you doing this ThirdParty Management project?

189. Change management vs. change leadership - what is the difference?

190. Will the risk plan be updated on a regular and frequent basis?

191. If there are vendors, have they signed off on the ThirdParty Management project Plan?

192. Is your organization structure appropriate for the

ThirdParty Management projects size and complexity?

193. Have you been able to thoroughly document the ThirdParty Management projects assumptions and constraints?

194. Is there a Quality Assurance Plan documented and filed?

195. Has everyone approved the ThirdParty Management projects scope statement?

196. Will the risk status be reported to management on a regular and frequent basis?

197. Is this process communicated to the customer and team members?

198. How will you verify the accuracy of the work of the ThirdParty Management project, and what constitutes acceptance of the deliverables?

199. Are the meetings set up to have assigned note takers that will add action/issues to the issue list?

200. Any new risks introduced or old risks impacted. Are there issues that could affect the existing requirements for the result, service, or product if the scope changes?

201. If there is an independent oversight contractor, have they signed off on the ThirdParty Management project Plan?

202. What should you drop in order to add something new?

2.7 Assumption and Constraint Log: ThirdParty Management

203. Are you meeting your customers expectations consistently?

204. What other teams / processes would be impacted by changes to the current process, and how?

205. Have all involved stakeholders and work groups committed to the ThirdParty Management project?

206. Is this process still needed?

207. How relevant is this attribute to this ThirdParty Management project or audit?

208. What to do at recovery?

209. Are there procedures in place to effectively manage interdependencies with other ThirdParty Management projects / systems?

210. Has a ThirdParty Management project Communications Plan been developed?

211. What is positive about the current process?

212. Contradictory information between document sections?

213. Are requirements management tracking tools and procedures in place?

214. After observing execution of process, is it in compliance with the documented Plan?

215. What worked well?

216. Would known impacts serve as impediments?

217. Have adequate resources been provided by management to ensure ThirdParty Management project success?

218. Are best practices and metrics employed to identify issues, progress, performance, etc.?

219. Is there adequate stakeholder participation for the vetting of requirements definition, changes and management?

220. What do you log?

221. How many ThirdParty Management project staff does this specific process affect?

2.8 Work Breakdown Structure: ThirdParty Management

222. How big is a work-package?

223. When does it have to be done?

224. Is the work breakdown structure (wbs) defined and is the scope of the ThirdParty Management project clear with assigned deliverable owners?

225. Why would you develop a Work Breakdown Structure?

226. Who has to do it?

227. Can you make it?

228. How many levels?

229. Why is it useful?

230. What is the probability that the ThirdParty Management project duration will exceed xx weeks?

231. Do you need another level?

232. What has to be done?

233. When do you stop?

234. What is the probability of completing the ThirdParty Management project in less that xx days?

235. How much detail?

236. Where does it take place?

237. How far down?

238. When would you develop a Work Breakdown Structure?

2.9 WBS Dictionary: ThirdParty Management

239. Are the procedures for identifying indirect costs to incurring organizations, indirect cost pools, and allocating the costs from the pools to the contracts formally documented?

240. Are time-phased budgets established for planning and control of level of effort activity by category of resource; for example, type of manpower and/or material?

241. Are data being used by managers in an effective manner to ascertain ThirdParty Management project or functional status, to identify reasons or significant variance, and to initiate appropriate corrective action?

242. Are overhead cost budgets (or ThirdParty Management projections) established on a facility-wide basis at least annually for the life of the contract?

243. Actual cost of work performed?

244. Budgets assigned to control accounts?

245. Contemplated overhead expenditure for each period based on the best information currently available?

246. Is future work which cannot be planned in detail subdivided to the extent practicable for budgeting and scheduling purposes?

247. Is the entire contract planned in time-phased control accounts to the extent practicable?

248. Are management actions taken to reduce indirect costs when there are significant adverse variances?

249. Are internal budgets for authorized, and not priced changes based on the contractors resource plan for accomplishing the work?

250. Are current work performance indicators and goals relatable to original goals as modified by contractual changes, replanning, and reprogramming actions?

251. Does the contractor have procedures which permit identification of recurring or non-recurring costs as necessary?

252. Does the accounting system provide a basis for auditing records of direct costs chargeable to the contract?

253. Are estimates of costs at completion generated in a rational, consistent manner?

254. Are the contractors estimates of costs at completion reconcilable with cost data reported to us?

255. Does the contractors system provide unit or lot costs when applicable?

256. Are meaningful indicators identified for use

in measuring the status of cost and schedule performance?

2.10 Schedule Management Plan: ThirdParty Management

257. Has a capability assessment been conducted?

258. Is a process defined to measure the performance of the schedule management process itself?

259. Is the assigned ThirdParty Management project manager a PMP (Certified ThirdParty Management project manager) and experienced?

260. Does the time ThirdParty Management projection include an amount for contingencies (time reserves)?

261. What strengths do you have?

262. What tools and techniques will be used to estimate activity durations?

263. Does the schedule have reasonable float?

264. Has the ims content been baselined and is it adequately controlled?

265. Does the resource management plan include a personnel development plan?

266. Are multiple estimation methods being employed?

267. Are adequate resources provided for the quality

assurance function?

268. Which status reports are received per the ThirdParty Management project Plan?

269. Is the steering committee active in ThirdParty Management project oversight?

270. Is a pmo (ThirdParty Management project management office) in place and provide oversight to the ThirdParty Management project?

271. Will rolling way planning be used?

272. Staffing Requirements?

273. Were ThirdParty Management project team members involved in detailed estimating and scheduling?

274. Are assumptions being identified, recorded, analyzed, qualified and closed?

2.11 Activity List: ThirdParty Management

275. Is infrastructure setup part of your ThirdParty Management project?

276. What is your organizations history in doing similar activities?

277. How detailed should a ThirdParty Management project get?

278. Who will perform the work?

279. How do you determine the late start (LS) for each activity?

280. The wbs is developed as part of a joint planning session. and how do you know that youhave done this right?

281. Can you determine the activity that must finish, before this activity can start?

282. When will the work be performed?

283. How should ongoing costs be monitored to try to keep the ThirdParty Management project within budget?

284. Where will it be performed?

285. In what sequence?

286. How can the ThirdParty Management project be displayed graphically to better visualize the activities?

287. How much slack is available in the ThirdParty Management project?

288. Is there anything planned that does not need to be here?

289. What will be performed?

290. For other activities, how much delay can be tolerated?

291. What went well?

292. Should you include sub-activities?

2.12 Activity Attributes: ThirdParty Management

293. How else could the items be grouped?

294. How do you manage time?

295. Where else does it apply?

296. How difficult will it be to do specific activities on this ThirdParty Management project?

297. Resources to accomplish the work?

298. Activity: what is Missing?

299. How many resources do you need to complete the work scope within a limit of X number of days?

300. Does your organization of the data change its meaning?

301. Has management defined a definite timeframe for the turnaround or ThirdParty Management project window?

302. How difficult will it be to complete specific activities on this ThirdParty Management project?

303. What is the general pattern here?

304. What is missing?

305. Would you consider either of corresponding activities an outlier?

306. Why?

307. Are the required resources available or need to be acquired?

308. What went right?

309. Do you feel very comfortable with your prediction?

2.13 Milestone List: ThirdParty Management

310. How soon can the activity start?

311. Timescales, deadlines and pressures?

312. What are your competitors vulnerabilities?

313. How late can the activity finish?

314. How difficult will it be to do specific activities on this ThirdParty Management project?

315. Vital contracts and partners?

316. Obstacles faced?

317. How late can each activity be finished and started?

318. Identify critical paths (one or more) and which activities are on the critical path?

319. Can you derive how soon can the whole ThirdParty Management project finish?

320. Competitive advantages?

321. Marketing - reach, distribution, awareness?

322. Describe the industry you are in and the market growth opportunities. What is the market for your

technology, product or service?

323. How will the milestone be verified?

324. What specific improvements did you make to the ThirdParty Management project proposal since the previous time?

2.14 Network Diagram: ThirdParty Management

325. What are the Major Administrative Issues?

326. What activities must occur simultaneously with this activity?

327. Where do schedules come from?

328. If x is long, what would be the completion time if you break x into two parallel parts of y weeks and z weeks?

329. Planning: who, how long, what to do?

330. Where do you schedule uncertainty time?

331. What is the probability of completing the ThirdParty Management project in less that xx days?

332. Are you on time?

333. How difficult will it be to do specific activities on this ThirdParty Management project?

334. Are the required resources available?

335. What is the lowest cost to complete this ThirdParty Management project in xx weeks?

336. If the ThirdParty Management project network diagram cannot change and you have extra personnel

resources, what is the BEST thing to do?

337. Are the gantt chart and/or network diagram updated periodically and used to assess the overall ThirdParty Management project timetable?

338. Why must you schedule milestones, such as reviews, throughout the ThirdParty Management project?

339. What can be done concurrently?

340. What controls the start and finish of a job?

341. What activities must follow this activity?

342. What must be completed before an activity can be started?

2.15 Activity Resource Requirements: ThirdParty Management

343. Do you use tools like decomposition and rolling-wave planning to produce the activity list and other outputs?

344. When does monitoring begin?

345. Other support in specific areas?

346. Are there unresolved issues that need to be addressed?

347. Organizational Applicability?

348. What are constraints that you might find during the Human Resource Planning process?

349. How many signatures do you require on a check and does this match what is in your policy and procedures?

350. What is the Work Plan Standard?

351. Time for overtime?

352. How do you handle petty cash?

353. Anything else?

354. Why do you do that?

355. Which logical relationship does the PDM use most often?

2.16 Resource Breakdown Structure: ThirdParty Management

356. How should the information be delivered?

357. Why is this important?

358. Who delivers the information?

359. What are the requirements for resource data?

360. How difficult will it be to do specific activities on this ThirdParty Management project?

361. What defines a successful ThirdParty Management project?

362. Which resources should be in the resource pool?

363. What is each stakeholders desired outcome for the ThirdParty Management project?

364. Goals for the ThirdParty Management project. What is each stakeholders desired outcome for the ThirdParty Management project?

365. Any changes from stakeholders?

366. Who is allowed to see what data about which resources?

367. Who will be used as a ThirdParty Management project team member?

368. What is the difference between % Complete and % work?

369. Changes based on input from stakeholders?

370. Why time management?

371. What is the number one predictor of a groups productivity?

372. Is predictive resource analysis being done?

2.17 Activity Duration Estimates: ThirdParty Management

373. Are contractor costs, schedule and technical performance monitored throughout the ThirdParty Management project?

374. What is pmp certification, and why do you think the number of people earning it has grown so much in the past ten years?

375. Who has the PRIMARY responsibility to solve this problem?

376. Briefly summarize the work done by Maslow, Herzberg, McClellan, McGregor, Ouchi, Thamhain and Wilemon, and Covey. How do theories relate to ThirdParty Management project management?

377. What is the duration of the critical path for this ThirdParty Management project?

378. Why should ThirdParty Management project managers strive to make jobs look easy?

379. Which skills do you think are most important for an information technology ThirdParty Management project manager?

380. Which does one need in order to complete schedule development?

381. Which is correct?

382. Describe ThirdParty Management project integration management in your own words. How does ThirdParty Management project integration management relate to the ThirdParty Management project life cycle, stakeholders, and the other ThirdParty Management project management knowledge areas?

383. Is a ThirdParty Management project charter created once a ThirdParty Management project is formally recognized?

384. What is done after activity duration estimation?

385. What is involved in the solicitation process?

386. Will it help promote wellness at your organization and reduce insurance costs?

387. What does it mean to take a systems view of a ThirdParty Management project?

388. Are many products available?

389. How does poking fun at technical professionals communications skills impact the industry and educational programs?

2.18 Duration Estimating Worksheet: ThirdParty Management

390. What utility impacts are there?

391. What is an Average ThirdParty Management project?

392. Why estimate time and cost?

393. Will the ThirdParty Management project collaborate with the local community and leverage resources?

394. What questions do you have?

395. When do the individual activities need to start and finish?

396. When does your organization expect to be able to complete it?

397. Do any colleagues have experience with your organization and/or RFPs?

398. What is cost and ThirdParty Management project cost management?

399. Science = process: remember the scientific method?

400. What are the critical bottleneck activities?

401. How can the ThirdParty Management project be displayed graphically to better visualize the activities?

402. Is a construction detail attached (to aid in explanation)?

403. Define the work as completely as possible. What work will be included in the ThirdParty Management project?

404. What work will be included in the ThirdParty Management project?

405. Why estimate costs?

406. Is this operation cost effective?

2.19 Project Schedule: ThirdParty Management

407. To what degree is do you feel the entire team was committed to the ThirdParty Management project schedule?

408. How much slack is available in the ThirdParty Management project?

409. It allows the ThirdParty Management project to be delivered on schedule. How Do you Use Schedules?

410. Why do you think schedule issues often cause the most conflicts on ThirdParty Management projects?

411. Your best shot for providing estimations how complex/how much work does the activity require?

412. How effectively were issues able to be resolved without impacting the ThirdParty Management project Schedule or Budget?

413. Are there activities that came from a template or previous ThirdParty Management project that are not applicable on this phase of this ThirdParty Management project?

414. Why is this particularly bad?

415. Meet requirements?

416. How do you know that youhave done this right?

417. Was the ThirdParty Management project schedule reviewed by all stakeholders and formally accepted?

418. Should you have a test for each code module?

419. How can you minimize or control changes to ThirdParty Management project schedules?

420. Did the final product meet or exceed user expectations?

421. How can you address that situation?

422. Is there a Schedule Management Plan that establishes the criteria and activities for developing, monitoring and controlling the ThirdParty Management project schedule?

423. Why do you need schedules?

2.20 Cost Management Plan: ThirdParty Management

424. Are estimating assumptions and constraints captured?

425. Is it standard practice to formally commit stakeholders to the ThirdParty Management project via agreements?

426. Resources – how will human resources be scheduled during each phase of the ThirdParty Management project?

427. Have ThirdParty Management project team accountabilities & responsibilities been clearly defined?

428. What would you do differently what did not work?

429. Are changes in scope (deliverable commitments) agreed to by all affected groups & individuals?

430. Has a structured approach been used to break work effort into manageable components (WBS)?

431. Were the budget estimates reasonable?

432. Schedule variances – how will schedule variances be identified and corrected?

433. Will the earned value reporting interface

between time and cost management?

434. Does the ThirdParty Management project have a Statement of Work?

435. Have external dependencies been captured in the schedule?

436. Cost estimate preparation – What cost estimates will be prepared during the ThirdParty Management project phases?

437. Do ThirdParty Management project teams & team members report on status / activities / progress?

2.21 Activity Cost Estimates: ThirdParty Management

438. How do you manage cost?

439. Can you delete activities or make them inactive?

440. Can you change your activities?

441. What areas does the group agree are the biggest success on the ThirdParty Management project?

442. What areas were overlooked on this ThirdParty Management project?

443. What do you want to know about the stay to know if costs were inappropriately high or low?

444. Were decisions made in a timely manner?

445. How many activities should you have?

446. What are the audit requirements?

447. Does the estimator have experience?

448. When do you enter into PPM?

449. Were the costs or charges reasonable?

450. Were you satisfied with the work?

451. Certification of actual expenditures?

452. What is the activity inventory?

453. In which phase of the acquisition process cycle does source qualifications reside?

454. How Award?

455. One way to define activities is to consider how organization employees describe jobs to families and friends. You basically want to know, What do you do?

456. What makes a good expected result statement?

2.22 Cost Estimating Worksheet: ThirdParty Management

457. Identify the timeframe necessary to monitor progress and collect data to determine how the selected measure has changed?

458. Who is best positioned to know and assist in identifying corresponding factors?

459. What is the purpose of estimating?

460. What info is needed?

461. What is the estimated labor cost today based upon this information?

462. Will the ThirdParty Management project collaborate with the local community and leverage resources?

463. How will the results be shared and to whom?

464. What happens to any remaining funds not used?

465. Does the ThirdParty Management project provide innovative ways for stakeholders to overcome obstacles or deliver better outcomes?

466. Can a trend be established from historical performance data on the selected measure and are the criteria for using trend analysis or forecasting methods met?

467. What additional ThirdParty Management project(s) could be initiated as a result of this ThirdParty Management project?

468. Is it feasible to establish a control group arrangement?

469. What can be included?

470. Value pocket identification & quantification what are value pockets?

471. What costs are to be estimated?

472. Is the ThirdParty Management project responsive to community need?

473. What will others want?

474. Ask: are others positioned to know, are others credible, and will others cooperate?

2.23 Cost Baseline: ThirdParty Management

475. Is request in line with priorities?

476. Has the actual cost of the ThirdParty Management project (or ThirdParty Management project phase) been tallied and compared to the approved budget?

477. Does the suggested change request represent a desired enhancement to the products functionality?

478. Impact to environment?

479. Has the ThirdParty Management projected annual cost to operate and maintain the product(s) or service(s) been approved and funded?

480. How likely is it to go wrong?

481. Have the lessons learned been filed with the ThirdParty Management project Management Office?

482. For what purpose ?

483. Where do changes come from?

484. Has the appropriate access to relevant data and analysis capability been granted?

485. Have you identified skills that are missing from your team?

486. Have all approved changes to the schedule baseline been identified and impact on the ThirdParty Management project documented?

487. On time?

488. Is the cr within ThirdParty Management project scope?

489. Has the ThirdParty Management project (or ThirdParty Management project phase) been evaluated against each objective established in the product description and Integrated ThirdParty Management project Plan?

2.24 Quality Management Plan: ThirdParty Management

490. What are your organizations current levels and trends for the already stated measures related to customer satisfaction/ dissatisfaction and product/ service performance?

491. How does your organization ensure the quality, reliability, and user-friendliness of its hardware and software?

492. How is staff trained?

493. How are data handled when a test is not run per specification?

494. Is staff trained on the software technologies that are being used on the ThirdParty Management project?

495. How does your organization establish and maintain customer relationships?

496. How does your organization determine the requirements and product/service features important to customers?

497. Does the program use other agents to collect samples?

498. How do you decide who is responsible for signing the data reports?

499. Does the ThirdParty Management project have a formal ThirdParty Management project Plan?

500. How will you know that a change is actually an improvement?

501. Do you keep back-up copies of any data?

502. How do senior leaders create an environment that encourages learning and innovation?

503. What process do you use to minimize errors, defects, and rework?

504. Is there a procedure for this process?

505. Does the plan conform to standards?

506. How is staff trained in procedures?

507. What is the Quality Management Plan?

508. Does a prospective decision remain the same regardless of what the data show is?

2.25 Quality Metrics: ThirdParty Management

509. Were number of defects identified?

510. Have risk areas been identified?

511. Where is quality now?

512. How do you measure?

513. How should customers provide input?

514. Has trace of defects been initiated?

515. What documentation is required?

516. Which are the right metrics to use?

517. What makes a visualization memorable?

518. What method of measurement do you use?

519. Which report did you use to create the data you are submitting?

520. Should a modifier be included?

521. What is the CMS Benchmark?

522. What are you trying to accomplish?

523. The metrics–what is being considered?

524. How exactly do you define when differences exist?

525. Is material complete (and does it meet the standards)?

526. When will the Final Guidance will be issued?

527. Is quality culture a competitive advantage?

2.26 Process Improvement Plan: ThirdParty Management

528. What is the test-cycle concept?

529. What actions are needed to address the problems and achieve the goals?

530. Does your process ensure quality?

531. Where are you now?

532. If a process improvement framework is being used, which elements will help the problems and goals listed?

533. Modeling current processes is great, and will you ever see a return on that investment?

534. What personnel are the sponsors for that initiative?

535. What personnel are the champions for the initiative?

536. What is the return on investment?

537. To elicit goal statements, do you ask a question such as, What do you want to achieve?

538. What lessons have you learned so far?

539. Are you making progress on the goals?

540. Where do you want to be?

541. Why do you want to achieve the goal?

542. What personnel are the coaches for your initiative?

543. What makes people good SPI coaches?

544. Are there forms and procedures to collect and record the data?

545. Are you meeting the quality standards?

2.27 Responsibility Assignment Matrix: ThirdParty Management

546. Are all elements of indirect expense identified to overhead cost budgets of ThirdParty Management projections?

547. What are the constraints?

548. What cost control tool do many experts say is crucial to ThirdParty Management project management?

549. Incurrence of actual indirect costs in excess of budgets, by element of expense?

550. Are work packages assigned to performing organizations?

551. Are all authorized tasks assigned to identified organizational elements?

552. Is it safe to say you can handle more work or that some tasks you are supposed to do arent worth doing?

553. Do you know how your people are allocated?

554. Are the overhead pools formally and adequately identified?

555. Are records maintained to show how undistributed budgets are controlled?

556. Who is the ThirdParty Management project Manager?

557. How do you manage human resources?

558. Is cost and schedule performance measurement done in a consistent, systematic manner?

559. Why cost benefit analysis?

560. Changes in the current direct and ThirdParty Management projected base?

561. Do you need to convince people that its well worth the time and effort?

562. Will too many Communicating responsibilities tangle the ThirdParty Management project in unnecessary communications?

563. Is work progressively subdivided into detailed work packages as requirements are defined?

564. Are people encouraged to bring up issues?

2.28 Roles and Responsibilities: ThirdParty Management

565. What are your major roles and responsibilities in the area of performance measurement and assessment?

566. Are ThirdParty Management project team roles and responsibilities identified and documented?

567. What should you do now to ensure that you are meeting all expectations of your current position?

568. Be specific; avoid generalities. Thank you and great work alone are insufficient. What exactly do you appreciate and why?

569. Are ThirdParty Management project team roles and responsibilities identified and documented?

570. How is your work-life balance?

571. Required skills, knowledge, experience?

572. Accountabilities: what are the roles and responsibilities of individual team members?

573. What expectations were met?

574. What areas of supervision are challenging for you?

575. Does the team have access to and ability to use

data analysis tools?

576. Are governance roles and responsibilities documented?

577. What is working well?

578. Is the data complete?

579. Implementation of actions: Who are the responsible units?

580. Concern: where are you limited or have no authority, where you can not influence?

581. Key conclusions and recommendations. Are conclusions and recommendations relevant and acceptable?

582. What is working well within your organizations performance management system?

2.29 Human Resource Management Plan: ThirdParty Management

583. What skills, knowledge and experiences are required?

584. Have ThirdParty Management project management standards and procedures been identified / established and documented?

585. Are risk oriented checklists used during risk identification?

586. Are the right people being attracted and retained to meet the future challenges?

587. Are action items captured and managed?

588. Are the appropriate IT resources adequate to meet planned commitments?

589. Were stakeholders aware and supportive of the principles and practices of modern cost estimation?

590. Have all documents been archived in a ThirdParty Management project repository for each release?

591. Is there a set of procedures to capture, analyze and act on quality metrics?

592. Have adequate resources been provided by management to ensure ThirdParty Management project success?

593. Are written status reports provided on a designated frequent basis?

594. Are the ThirdParty Management project team members located locally to the users/stakeholders?

595. Is there an onboarding process in place?

596. What is this ThirdParty Management project aiming to achieve?

597. Has a ThirdParty Management project Communications Plan been developed?

598. Is this ThirdParty Management project carried out in partnership with other groups/organizations?

599. Have all unresolved risks been documented?

600. Have stakeholder accountabilities & responsibilities been clearly defined?

2.30 Communications Management Plan: ThirdParty Management

601. Is there an important stakeholder who is actively opposed and will not receive messages?

602. What steps can you take for a positive relationship?

603. Who is responsible?

604. How were corresponding initiatives successful?

605. What help do you and your team need from the stakeholder?

606. What is the stakeholders level of authority?

607. Who to share with?

608. How is this initiative related to other portfolios, programs, or ThirdParty Management projects?

609. Do you then often overlook a key stakeholder or stakeholder group?

610. Are there too many who have an interest in some aspect of your work?

611. Who have you worked with in past, similar initiatives?

612. Who is involved as you identify stakeholders?

613. In your work, how much time is spent on stakeholder identification?

614. Are the stakeholders getting the information others need, are others consulted, are concerns addressed?

615. Who were proponents/opponents?

616. Who is the stakeholder?

617. Who will use or be affected by the result of a ThirdParty Management project?

618. What to know?

619. What to learn?

620. Timing: when do the effects of the communication take place?

2.31 Risk Management Plan: ThirdParty Management

621. Maximize short-term return on investment?

622. What is the probability the risk avoidance strategy will be successful?

623. Methodology: how will risk management be performed on this ThirdParty Management project?

624. How is the audit profession changing?

625. How quickly does this item need to be resolved?

626. Does the customer have a solid idea of what is required?

627. Why do you need to manage ThirdParty Management project Risk?

628. Are people attending meetings and doing work?

629. Monitoring -what factors can you track that will enable you to determine if the risk is becoming more or less likely?

630. Are the participants able to keep up with the workload?

631. Are there risks to human health or the environment that need to be controlled or mitigated?

632. What is the impact to the ThirdParty Management project if the item is not resolved in a timely fashion?

633. How much risk protection can you afford?

634. Who/what can assist?

635. Risk categories: what are the main categories of risks that should be addressed on this ThirdParty Management project?

636. How can you fix it?

637. Are there new risks that mitigation strategies might introduce?

638. For software; are compilers and code generators available and suitable for the product to be built?

639. Is there additional information that would make you more confident about your analysis?

2.32 Risk Register: ThirdParty Management

640. What is a Risk?

641. What further options might be available for responding to the risk?

642. When would you develop a risk register?

643. What is a Community Risk Register?

644. Are implemented controls working as others should?

645. What is the probability and impact of the risk occurring?

646. What is the reason for current performance gaps and do the risks and opportunities identified previously account for this?

647. What can be done about it?

648. Severity Prediction?

649. Who is going to do it?

650. Assume the event happens, what is the Most Likely impact?

651. What evidence do you have to justify the likelihood score of the risk (audit, incident report,

claim, complaints, inspection, internal review)?

652. Can the likelihood and impact of failing to achieve corresponding recommendations and action plans be assessed?

653. What are the main aims, objectives of the policy, strategy, or service and the intended outcomes?

654. Financial risk -can your organization afford to undertake the ThirdParty Management project?

655. Who is accountable?

656. Who needs to know about this?

657. Are there any gaps in the evidence?

2.33 Probability and Impact Assessment: ThirdParty Management

658. Why has this particular mode of contracting been chosen?

659. Who will be in command to monitor and control the performance of the consortium members (consortium leader/client)?

660. What risks are necessary to achieve success?

661. Have you ascribed a level of confidence to every critical technical objective?

662. Are the risk data complete?

663. Is the delay in one subThirdParty Management project going to affect another?

664. Do you use any methods to analyze risks?

665. How are you working with risks?

666. Which functions, departments, and activities of your organization are going to be affected?

667. How solid is the ThirdParty Management projection of competitive reaction?

668. Are the facilities, expertise, resources, and management know-how available to handle the situation?

669. Who should be responsible for the monitoring and tracking of the indicators you have identified?

670. Are ThirdParty Management project requirements stable?

671. Risk data quality assessment - what is the quality of the data used to determine or assess the risk?

672. Is the customer willing to participate in reviews?

673. Will there be an increase in the political conservatism?

674. How do you maximize short term return on investment?

675. How is risk handled within this ThirdParty Management project organization?

676. Are enough people available?

677. What are the current requirements of the customer?

2.34 Probability and Impact Matrix: ThirdParty Management

678. Several experts are offsite, and wish to be included. How can this be done?

679. What would you do differently?

680. Which phase of the ThirdParty Management project do you take part in?

681. How well is the risk understood?

682. What is the likelihood?

683. Do you have a consistent repeatable process that is actually used?

684. My ThirdParty Management project leader has suddenly left your organization, what do you do?

685. Are staff committed for the duration of the ThirdParty Management project?

686. Can you avoid altogether some things that might go wrong?

687. How risk averse are you?

688. What should be the gestation period for the ThirdParty Management project with this technology?

689. What has the ThirdParty Management project

manager forgotten to do?

690. How will economic events and trends likely affect the ThirdParty Management project?

691. What lifestyle shifts might occur in society?

692. Are there alternative opinions/solutions/ processes you should explore?

693. What is the likelihood of a breakthrough?

694. Is the customer willing to establish rapid communication links with the developer?

695. Do others match with the clients requirement?

2.35 Risk Data Sheet: ThirdParty Management

696. Potential for recurrence?

697. What were the Causes that contributed?

698. How can hazards be reduced?

699. Whom do you serve (customers)?

700. What is the chance that it will happen?

701. What if client refuses?

702. What are the main opportunities available to you that you should grab while you can?

703. What are you trying to achieve (Objectives)?

704. Are new hazards created?

705. Risk of what?

706. What will be the consequences if it happens?

707. Type of risk identified?

708. What is the environment within which you operate (social trends, economic, community values, broad based participation, national directions etc.)?

709. Has a sensitivity analysis been carried out?

710. During work activities could hazards exist?

711. What will be the consequences if the risk happens?

712. What are your core values?

713. What are the main threats to your existence?

2.36 Procurement Management Plan: ThirdParty Management

714. Pareto diagrams, statistical sampling, flow charting or trend analysis used quality monitoring?

715. Are mitigation strategies identified?

716. Does a documented ThirdParty Management project organizational policy & plan (i.e. governance model) exist?

717. Has the scope management document been updated and distributed to help prevent scope creep?

718. What is a ThirdParty Management project Management Plan?

719. Has ThirdParty Management project success criteria been defined?

720. Was an original risk assessment/risk management plan completed?

721. Are there checklists created to determine if all quality processes are followed?

722. What are your quality assurance overheads?

723. Are corrective actions and variances reported?

724. How will the duration of the ThirdParty Management project influence your decisions?

725. Is a stakeholder management plan in place that covers topics?

726. Are trade-offs between accepting the risk and mitigating the risk identified?

727. Based on your ThirdParty Management project communication management plan, what worked well?

728. Was your organizations estimating methodology being used and followed?

729. Is pert / critical path or equivalent methodology being used?

730. Were ThirdParty Management project team members involved in detailed estimating and scheduling?

2.37 Source Selection Criteria: ThirdParty Management

731. What are the special considerations for preaward debriefings?

732. Is there collaboration among your evaluators?

733. Do you want to wait until all offerors have been evaluated?

734. Are responses to considerations adequate?

735. Do you prepare an independent cost estimate?

736. What is cost analysis and when should it be performed?

737. How and when do you enter into ThirdParty Management project Procurement Management?

738. Why promote competition?

739. What risks were identified in the proposals?

740. How are clarifications and communications appropriately used?

741. What evidence should be provided regarding proposal evaluations?

742. How can the methods of publicizing the buy be tailored to yield more effective price competition?

743. How should the oral presentations be handled?

744. When and what information can be considered with offerors regarding past performance?

745. Does the evaluation of any change include an impact analysis; how will the change affect the scope, time, cost, and quality of the goods or services being provided?

746. What past performance information should be requested?

747. How do you facilitate evaluation against published criteria?

748. What should be considered?

749. Can you reasonably estimate total organization requirements for the coming year?

750. When is it appropriate to issue a DRFP?

2.38 Stakeholder Management Plan: ThirdParty Management

751. Does the ThirdParty Management project have a formal ThirdParty Management project Plan?

752. Who will be responsible for managing and maintaining the Issues Register?

753. Are cause and effect determined for risks when they occur?

754. Have reserves been created to address risks?

755. How many ThirdParty Management project staff does this specific process affect?

756. Have ThirdParty Management project success criteria been defined?

757. What is meant by activity dependencies and how do they relate to network diagramming?

758. Is there a Steering Committee in place?

759. Are there nonconformance issues?

760. Are there processes in place to ensure internal consistency between the source code components?

761. Have all involved ThirdParty Management project stakeholders and work groups committed to the ThirdParty Management project?

762. Describe the process that will be used to design, develop, review, accept, distribute and change outputs. Will all outputs delivered by the ThirdParty Management project follow the same process?

763. Are ThirdParty Management project leaders committed to this ThirdParty Management project full time?

764. Are the people assigned to the ThirdParty Management project sufficiently qualified?

765. Is there general agreement & acceptance of the current status and progress of the ThirdParty Management project?

766. Are there unnecessary steps that are creating bottlenecks and/or causing people to wait?

2.39 Change Management Plan: ThirdParty Management

767. What are the training strategies?

768. Where will the funds come from?

769. What relationships will change?

770. Has a training need analysis been carried out?

771. Which relationships will change?

772. Who will be the change levers?

773. When developing your communication plan do you address : When should the given message be communicated?

774. What does a resilient organization look like?

775. What new roles are needed?

776. Is it the same for each of the business units?

777. When should a given message be communicated?

778. How do you gain sponsors buy-in to the communication plan?

779. Who is the target audience of the piece of information?

780. Has the training provider been established?

781. How badly can information be misinterpreted?

782. What are the specific target groups/audiences that will be impacted by this change?

783. Will you need new processes?

784. Readiness -what is a successful end state?

785. What would be an estimate of the total cost for the activities required to carry out the change initiative?

786. What is the worst thing that can happen if you chose not to communicate this information?

3.0 Executing Process Group: ThirdParty Management

787. How does a ThirdParty Management project life cycle differ from a product life cycle?

788. What areas were overlooked on this ThirdParty Management project?

789. Were sponsors and decision makers available when needed outside regularly scheduled meetings?

790. Will additional funds be needed for hardware or software?

791. What areas does the group agree are the biggest success on the ThirdParty Management project?

792. Would you rate yourself as being risk-averse, risk-neutral, or risk-seeking?

793. How will you avoid scope creep?

794. How do you measure difficulty?

795. What will you do to minimize the impact should a risk event occur?

796. What were things that you did very well and want to do the same again on the next ThirdParty Management project?

797. On which process should team members spend

the most time?

798. What were things that you did well, and could improve, and how?

799. How can you use Microsoft ThirdParty Management project and Excel to assist in ThirdParty Management project risk management?

800. What are the main types of goods and services being outsourced?

801. If a risk event occurs, what will you do?

802. Mitigate, what will you do to minimize the impact should a risk event occur?

803. Is activity definition the first process involved in ThirdParty Management project time management?

804. Are decisions made in a timely manner?

3.1 Team Member Status Report: ThirdParty Management

805. Is there evidence that staff is taking a more professional approach toward management of your organizations ThirdParty Management projects?

806. Are the attitudes of staff regarding ThirdParty Management project work improving?

807. Does every department have to have a ThirdParty Management project Manager on staff?

808. Are your organizations ThirdParty Management projects more successful over time?

809. The problem with Reward & Recognition Programs is that the truly deserving people all too often get left out. How can you make it practical?

810. Are the products of your organizations ThirdParty Management projects meeting customers objectives?

811. Will the staff do training or is that done by a third party?

812. Do you have an Enterprise ThirdParty Management project Management Office (EPMO)?

813. How will resource planning be done?

814. How much risk is involved?

815. How it is to be done?

816. How can you make it practical?

817. How does this product, good, or service meet the needs of the ThirdParty Management project and your organization as a whole?

818. What specific interest groups do you have in place?

819. Why is it to be done?

820. Does the product, good, or service already exist within your organization?

821. What is to be done?

822. Does your organization have the means (staff, money, contract, etc.) to produce or to acquire the product, good, or service?

823. When a teams productivity and success depend on collaboration and the efficient flow of information, what generally fails them?

3.2 Change Request: ThirdParty Management

824. Who is included in the change control team?

825. What are the basic mechanics of the Change Advisory Board (CAB)?

826. Are there requirements attributes that are strongly related to the occurrence of defects and failures?

827. Should a more thorough impact analysis be conducted?

828. What are the requirements for urgent changes?

829. How does your organization control changes before and after software is released to a customer?

830. How is the change documented (format, content, storage)?

831. How many lines of code must be changed to implement the change?

832. Are there requirements attributes that are strongly related to the complexity and size?

833. Is it feasible to use requirements attributes as predictors of reliability?

834. Why do you want to have a change control

system?

835. Have scm procedures for noting the change, recording it, and reporting it been followed?

836. Are there requirements attributes that can discriminate between high and low reliability?

837. What are the duties of the change control team?

838. How fast will change requests be approved?

839. What kind of information about the change request needs to be captured?

840. Will this change conflict with other requirements changes (e.g., lead to conflicting operational scenarios)?

841. How does a team identify the discrete elements of a configuration?

842. What should be regulated in a change control operating instruction?

3.3 Change Log: ThirdParty Management

843. When was the request submitted?

844. Will the ThirdParty Management project fail if the change request is not executed?

845. Who initiated the change request?

846. Is this a mandatory replacement?

847. How does this change affect the timeline of the schedule?

848. How does this change affect scope?

849. How does this relate to the standards developed for specific business processes?

850. Is the change request open, closed or pending?

851. Is the requested change request a result of changes in other ThirdParty Management project(s)?

852. Does the suggested change request seem to represent a necessary enhancement to the product?

853. When was the request approved?

854. Do the described changes impact on the integrity or security of the system?

855. Is the submitted change a new change or a modification of a previously approved change?

856. Is the change request within ThirdParty Management project scope?

857. Is the change backward compatible without limitations?

3.4 Decision Log: ThirdParty Management

858. What is the average size of your matters in an applicable measurement?

859. What eDiscovery problem or issue did your organization set out to fix or make better?

860. Is your opponent open to a non-traditional workflow, or will it likely challenge anything you do?

861. What makes you different or better than others companies selling the same thing?

862. Adversarial environment. is your opponent open to a non-traditional workflow, or will it likely challenge anything you do?

863. What alternatives/risks were considered?

864. How do you know when you are achieving it?

865. With whom was the decision shared or considered?

866. How consolidated and comprehensive a story can you tell by capturing currently available incident data in a central location and through a log of key decisions during an incident?

867. Who is the decisionmaker?

868. Decision-making process; how will the team make decisions?

869. Is everything working as expected?

870. Who will be given a copy of this document and where will it be kept?

871. How does provision of information, both in terms of content and presentation, influence acceptance of alternative strategies?

872. At what point in time does loss become unacceptable?

873. Meeting purpose; why does this team meet?

874. Which variables make a critical difference?

875. Behaviors; what are guidelines that the team has identified that will assist them with getting the most out of team meetings?

876. What is your overall strategy for quality control / quality assurance procedures?

877. What is the line where eDiscovery ends and document review begins?

3.5 Quality Audit: ThirdParty Management

878. How well do you think your organization engages with the outside community?

879. For each device to be reconditioned, are device specifications, such as appropriate engineering drawings, component specifications and software specifications, maintained?

880. Do the suppliers use a formal quality system?

881. How does your organization know that its systems for meeting staff extracurricular learning support requirements are appropriately effective and constructive?

882. How does your organization know that its staff support services planning and management systems are appropriately effective and constructive?

883. Are complaint files maintained?

884. How does your organization know that its range of activities are being reviewed as rigorously and constructively as they could be?

885. Does everyone know what they are supposed to be doing, how and why?

886. Is there a risk that information provided by management may not always be reliable?

887. How does your organization know that its system for recruiting the best staff possible are appropriately effective and constructive?

888. What does an analysis of your organizations staff profile suggest in terms of its planning, and how is this being addressed?

889. What is the collective experience of the team to be assigned to an audit?

890. How does your organization know that its information technology system is serving its needs as effectively and constructively as is appropriate?

891. How does your organization know that its staff placements are appropriately effective and constructive in relation to program-related learning outcomes?

892. How does your organization know that its Governance system is appropriately effective and constructive?

893. How does your organization ensure that equipment is appropriately maintained and producing valid results?

894. What does the organizarion look for in a Quality audit?

895. How does your organization know that its systems for communicating with and among staff are appropriately effective and constructive?

896. Are people allowed to contribute ideas?

897. How does your organization know that its system for managing intellectual property issues is appropriately effective, constructive and fair?

3.6 Team Directory: ThirdParty Management

898. Process decisions: is work progressing on schedule and per contract requirements?

899. Contract requirements complied with?

900. Is construction on schedule?

901. Who is the Sponsor?

902. Who should receive information (all stakeholders)?

903. Process decisions: are there any statutory or regulatory issues relevant to the timely execution of work?

904. Process decisions: are contractors adequately prosecuting the work?

905. Who will write the meeting minutes and distribute?

906. Do purchase specifications and configurations match requirements?

907. How do unidentified risks impact the outcome of the ThirdParty Management project?

908. Decisions: what could be done better to improve the quality of the constructed product?

909. Where will the product be used and/or delivered or built when appropriate?

910. How will the team handle changes?

911. Why is the work necessary?

912. When does information need to be distributed?

913. Who will talk to the customer?

914. Who will report ThirdParty Management project status to all stakeholders?

915. Who are the Team Members?

916. Does a ThirdParty Management project team directory list all resources assigned to the ThirdParty Management project?

917. How does the team resolve conflicts and ensure tasks are completed?

3.7 Team Operating Agreement: ThirdParty Management

918. Do you post any action items, due dates, and responsibilities on the team website?

919. What are the current caseload numbers in the unit?

920. Have you set the goals and objectives of the team?

921. Have you established procedures that team members can follow to work effectively together, such as a team operating agreement?

922. Did you determine the technology methods that best match the messages to be communicated?

923. Do you call or email participants to ensure understanding, follow-through and commitment to the meeting outcomes?

924. What is group supervision?

925. Reimbursements: how will the team members be reimbursed for expenses and time commitments?

926. Did you prepare participants for the next meeting?

927. Do you ensure that all participants know how to use the required technology?

928. Why does your organization want to participate in teaming?

929. What is a Virtual Team?

930. Confidentiality: how will confidential information be handled?

931. Are there more than two native languages represented by your team?

932. Do you begin with a question to engage everyone?

933. Do you upload presentation materials in advance and test the technology?

934. Are team roles clearly defined and accepted?

935. What are the boundaries (organizational or geographic) within which you operate?

936. Are there the right people on your team?

937. Communication protocols: how will the team communicate?

3.8 Team Performance Assessment: ThirdParty Management

938. To what degree do team members agree with the goals, relative importance, and the ways in which achievement will be measured?

939. Social categorization and intergroup behaviour: Does minimal intergroup discrimination make social identity more positive?

940. To what degree are the members clear on what they are individually responsible for and what they are jointly responsible for?

941. To what degree do team members frequently explore the teams purpose and its implications?

942. What are you doing specifically to develop the leaders around you?

943. Which situations call for a more extreme type of adaptiveness in which team members actually re-define roles?

944. To what degree are the skill areas critical to team performance present?

945. If you are worried about method variance before you collect data, what sort of design elements might you include to reduce or eliminate the threat of method variance?

946. To what degree are fresh input and perspectives systematically caught and added (for example, through information and analysis, new members, and senior sponsors)?

947. To what degree do the goals specify concrete team work products?

948. How much interpersonal friction is there in your team?

949. To what degree does the team possess adequate membership to achieve its ends?

950. If you have received criticism from reviewers that your work suffered from method variance, what was the circumstance?

951. To what degree will team members, individually and collectively, commit time to help themselves and others learn and develop skills?

952. What makes opportunities more or less obvious?

953. What are teams?

954. To what degree can team members vigorously define the teams purpose in considerations with others who are not part of the functioning team?

955. To what degree is there a sense that only the team can succeed?

956. To what degree does the teams purpose constitute a broader, deeper aspiration than just accomplishing short-term goals?

957. How hard did you try to make a good selection?

3.9 Team Member Performance Assessment: ThirdParty Management

958. How do you determine which data are the most important to use, analyze, or review?

959. Is there reluctance to join a team?

960. To what degree are sub-teams possible or necessary?

961. What future plans (e.g., modifications) do you have for your program?

962. To what degree do members articulate the goals beyond the team membership?

963. Is it critical or vital to the job?

964. What happens if a team member receives a Rating of Unsatisfactory?

965. How do you currently account for your results in the teams achievement?

966. How do you start collaborating?

967. How is your organizations Strategic Management System tied to performance measurement?

968. To what degree can team members meet frequently enough to accomplish the teams ends?

969. What are the staffs preferences for training on technology-based platforms?

970. Where can team members go for more detailed information on performance measurement and assessment?

971. Verify business objectives. Are they appropriate, and well-articulated?

972. What steps have you taken to improve performance?

973. Does adaptive training work?

974. Does platform-specific assessment information contribute to training placement or tailoring of instruction (e.g. aptitude-treatment interaction)?

975. To what degree are the relative importance and priority of the goals clear to all team members?

976. What is needed for effective data teams?

3.10 Issue Log: ThirdParty Management

977. What are the stakeholders interrelationships?

978. Is it a change in scope?

979. Are there potential barriers between the team and the stakeholder?

980. Why not more evaluators?

981. How do you manage communications?

982. What effort will a change need?

983. Why do you manage communications?

984. Do you feel a register helps?

985. What are the typical contents?

986. What steps can you take for positive relationships?

987. How often do you engage with stakeholders?

988. Which stakeholders are thought leaders, influences, or early adopters?

989. What is a change?

990. Is access to the Issue Log controlled?

991. Do you prepare stakeholder engagement plans?

4.0 Monitoring and Controlling Process Group: ThirdParty Management

992. What is the timeline for the ThirdParty Management project?

993. Who needs to be engaged upfront to ensure use of results?

994. Did the ThirdParty Management project team have the right skills?

995. What resources (both financial and non-financial) are available/needed?

996. Is there sufficient time allotted between the general system design and the detailed system design phases?

997. How many potential communications channels exist on the ThirdParty Management project?

998. What do they need to know about the ThirdParty Management project?

999. How well did the chosen processes fit the needs of the ThirdParty Management project?

1000. What are the deliverables?

1001. Is the verbiage used appropriate and understandable?

1002. Where is the Risk in the ThirdParty Management project?

1003. When will the ThirdParty Management project be done?

1004. Are there areas that need improvement?

1005. What areas does the group agree are the biggest success on the ThirdParty Management project?

1006. Is there adequate validation on required fields?

1007. Measurable - are the targets measurable?

1008. Did it work?

1009. Based on your ThirdParty Management project communication management plan, what worked well?

1010. How is agile portfolio management done?

4.1 Project Performance Report: ThirdParty Management

1011. To what degree can all members engage in open and interactive considerations?

1012. What is the PRS?

1013. To what degree can the team measure progress against specific goals?

1014. To what degree does the information network provide individuals with the information they require?

1015. To what degree do team members feel that the purpose of the team is important, if not exciting?

1016. To what degree do all members feel responsible for all agreed-upon measures?

1017. To what degree do individual skills and abilities match task demands?

1018. To what degree does the teams purpose contain themes that are particularly meaningful and memorable?

1019. To what degree can team members frequently and easily communicate with one another?

1020. To what degree will each member have the opportunity to advance his or her professional skills in all three of the above categories while contributing to the accomplishment of the teams purpose and goals?

1021. To what degree does the teams work approach provide opportunity for members to engage in open interaction?

1022. To what degree does the task meet individual needs?

1023. To what degree are the demands of the task compatible with and converge with the mission and functions of the formal organization?

1024. To what degree does the funding match the requirement?

1025. To what degree will the team ensure that all members equitably share the work essential to the success of the team?

1026. To what degree do team members articulate the teams work approach?

1027. What is the degree to which rules govern information exchange between groups?

4.2 Variance Analysis: ThirdParty Management

1028. Are there knowledgeable ThirdParty Management projections of future performance?

1029. Are there changes in the direct base to which overhead costs are allocated?

1030. How do you verify authorization to proceed with all authorized work?

1031. Is data disseminated to the contractors management timely, accurate, and usable?

1032. What is exceptional?

1033. How are material, labor, and overhead standards set?

1034. Are detailed work packages planned as far in advance as practicable?

1035. Budget versus actual. how does the monthly budget compare to actual experience?

1036. Are overhead cost budgets established for each department which has authority to incur overhead costs?

1037. How have the setting and use of standards changed over time?

1038. What is the performance to date and material commitment?

1039. Do you identify potential or actual budget-based and time-based schedule variances?

1040. Are the bases and rates for allocating costs from each indirect pool consistently applied?

1041. Wbs elements contractually specified for reporting of status to your organization (lowest level only)?

1042. Who is generally responsible for monitoring and taking action on variances?

1043. Historical experience?

1044. What should management do?

4.3 Earned Value Status: ThirdParty Management

1045. Where are your problem areas?

1046. When is it going to finish?

1047. Validation is a process of ensuring that the developed system will actually achieve the stakeholders desired outcomes; Are you building the right product? What do you validate?

1048. Are you hitting your ThirdParty Management projects targets?

1049. What is the unit of forecast value?

1050. How does this compare with other ThirdParty Management projects?

1051. How much is it going to cost by the finish?

1052. If earned value management (EVM) is so good in determining the true status of a ThirdParty Management project and ThirdParty Management project its completion, why is it that hardly any one uses it in information systems related ThirdParty Management projects?

1053. Verification is a process of ensuring that the developed system satisfies the stakeholders agreements and specifications; Are you building the product right? What do you verify?

1054. Earned value can be used in almost any ThirdParty Management project situation and in almost any ThirdParty Management project environment. it may be used on large ThirdParty Management projects, medium sized ThirdParty Management projects, tiny ThirdParty Management projects (in cut-down form), complex and simple ThirdParty Management projects and in any market sector. some people, of course, know all about earned value, they have used it for years - but perhaps not as effectively as they could have?

1055. Where is evidence-based earned value in your organization reported?

4.4 Risk Audit: ThirdParty Management

1056. Have top software and customer managers formally committed to support the ThirdParty Management project?

1057. Do you have written and signed agreements/ contracts in place for each paid staff member?

1058. Number of users of the product?

1059. Are risk management strategies documented?

1060. Will participants be required to sign a legally counselled waiver or risk disclaimer when entering an event?

1061. The halo effect in business risk audits: can strategic risk assessment bias auditor judgment about accounting details?

1062. Do you have an understanding of insurance claims processes?

1063. Are the software tools integrated with each other?

1064. Are all programs planned and conducted according to recognized safety standards?

1065. Does willful intent modify risk-based auditing?

1066. What are the strategic implications with clients when auditors focus audit resources based on business-level risks?

1067. Is the customer technically sophisticated in the product area?

1068. Do you promote education and training opportunities?

1069. Have staff received necessary training?

1070. What are the boundaries of the auditors responsibility for policing management fidelity?

1071. When your organization is entering into a major contract, does it seek legal advice?

1072. Level of preparation and skill?

1073. Are tool mentors available?

1074. Who is responsible for what?

1075. Are you willing to seek legal advice when required?

4.5 Contractor Status Report: ThirdParty Management

1076. Who can list a ThirdParty Management project as organization experience, your organization or a previous employee of your organization?

1077. Are there contractual transfer concerns?

1078. How is risk transferred?

1079. How does the proposed individual meet each requirement?

1080. What was the overall budget or estimated cost?

1081. If applicable; describe your standard schedule for new software version releases. Are new software version releases included in the standard maintenance plan?

1082. How long have you been using the services?

1083. What was the actual budget or estimated cost for your organizations services?

1084. What process manages the contracts?

1085. Describe how often regular updates are made to the proposed solution. Are corresponding regular updates included in the standard maintenance plan?

1086. What was the final actual cost?

1087. What is the average response time for answering a support call?

1088. What are the minimum and optimal bandwidth requirements for the proposed solution?

1089. What was the budget or estimated cost for your organizations services?

4.6 Formal Acceptance: ThirdParty Management

1090. How does your team plan to obtain formal acceptance on your ThirdParty Management project?

1091. Did the ThirdParty Management project manager and team act in a professional and ethical manner?

1092. Was the ThirdParty Management project goal achieved?

1093. Do you buy-in installation services?

1094. Have all comments been addressed?

1095. Who supplies data?

1096. What function(s) does it fill or meet?

1097. General estimate of the costs and times to complete the ThirdParty Management project?

1098. Do you buy pre-configured systems or build your own configuration?

1099. Was business value realized?

1100. What are the requirements against which to test, Who will execute?

1101. Did the ThirdParty Management project achieve

its MOV?

1102. What was done right?

1103. Who would use it?

1104. Was the client satisfied with the ThirdParty Management project results?

1105. What lessons were learned about your ThirdParty Management project management methodology?

1106. Was the ThirdParty Management project work done on time, within budget, and according to specification?

1107. What is the Acceptance Management Process?

1108. Do you perform formal acceptance or burn-in tests?

1109. Is formal acceptance of the ThirdParty Management project product documented and distributed?

5.0 Closing Process Group: ThirdParty Management

1110. Contingency planning. if a risk event occurs, what will you do?

1111. Is the ThirdParty Management project funded?

1112. What could have been improved?

1113. When will the ThirdParty Management project be done?

1114. What is the overall risk of the ThirdParty Management project to your organization?

1115. How will staff learn how to use the deliverables?

1116. Is there a clear cause and effect between the activity and the lesson learned?

1117. Will the ThirdParty Management project deliverable(s) replace a current asset or group of assets?

1118. What business situation is being addressed?

1119. What is the risk of failure to your organization?

1120. Did the ThirdParty Management project team have enough people to execute the ThirdParty Management project plan?

1121. Did you do what you said you were going to do?

1122. What do you need to do?

1123. What areas were overlooked on this ThirdParty Management project?

1124. What communication items need improvement?

1125. What were things that you need to improve?

1126. Did the delivered product meet the specified requirements and goals of the ThirdParty Management project?

5.1 Procurement Audit: ThirdParty Management

1127. Are proper financing arrangements taken?

1128. Were there no inconsistencies between the several tender documents?

1129. Could the bidders assess the economic risks the successful bidder would be responsible for, thus limiting the inclusion of extra charges for risk?

1130. Were there no material changes in the contract shortly after award?

1131. Are requisitions and other purchase requests batched to reduce the number of orders issued?

1132. Have guidelines incorporating the principles and objectives of a robust procurement practice been established?

1133. Is there no evidence that the consultants participating in the ThirdParty Management project design released information to contractors competing for the prime contract?

1134. Is it calculated whether aggregated procurement can be more cost-efficient?

1135. Are the supporting documents for payments voided or cancelled following payment?

1136. Relevance of the contract to the Internal Market?

1137. Did the additional works introduce minor or non-substantial changes to performance, as described in the contract documents?

1138. What are your ethical guidelines for public procurement?

1139. Was additional significant information supplied to all interested parties?

1140. Are tenders who do not comply with the requirements specified in the request for tenders rejected?

1141. Is sufficient evidence required for all disbursements (except nominal amounts)?

1142. Did the conditions included in the contract protect the risk of non-performance by the supplier and were there no conflicting provisions?

1143. Is an appropriated degree of standardization of goods and services respected?

1144. Are all checks pre-numbered?

1145. Are contract changes after awarding properly justified and executed?

1146. Which are main risks and controls of each phase?

5.2 Contract Close-Out: ThirdParty Management

1147. How is the contracting office notified of the automatic contract close-out?

1148. Was the contract type appropriate?

1149. Has each contract been audited to verify acceptance and delivery?

1150. Was the contract sufficiently clear so as not to result in numerous disputes and misunderstandings?

1151. Was the contract complete without requiring numerous changes and revisions?

1152. Change in knowledge?

1153. Have all contracts been closed?

1154. Parties: who is involved?

1155. Why Outsource?

1156. Have all contract records been included in the ThirdParty Management project archives?

1157. Are the signers the authorized officials?

1158. What happens to the recipient of services?

1159. Parties: Authorized?

1160. What is capture management?

1161. Change in attitude or behavior?

1162. How does it work?

1163. How/when used ?

1164. Have all contracts been completed?

1165. Change in circumstances?

1166. Have all acceptance criteria been met prior to final payment to contractors?

5.3 Project or Phase Close-Out: ThirdParty Management

1167. Who controlled the resources for the ThirdParty Management project?

1168. Planned completion date?

1169. How often did each stakeholder need an update?

1170. What was the preferred delivery mechanism?

1171. What were the desired outcomes?

1172. Does the lesson describe a function that would be done differently the next time?

1173. Who exerted influence that has positively affected or negatively impacted the ThirdParty Management project?

1174. Were cost budgets met?

1175. Have business partners been involved extensively, and what data was required for them?

1176. Who controlled key decisions that were made?

1177. What were the actual outcomes?

1178. What information is each stakeholder group interested in?

1179. What were the goals and objectives of the communications strategy for the ThirdParty Management project?

1180. What can you do better next time, and what specific actions can you take to improve?

1181. What was expected from each stakeholder?

1182. What process was planned for managing issues/risks?

1183. Was the user/client satisfied with the end product?

1184. What was learned?

1185. What are the marketing communication needs for each stakeholder?

5.4 Lessons Learned: ThirdParty Management

1186. Why does your organization need a lessons learned (LL) capability?

1187. How effective were the communications materials in providing and orienting team members about the details of the ThirdParty Management project?

1188. What is the economic growth rate?

1189. How well does the product or service the ThirdParty Management project produced meet the defined ThirdParty Management project requirements?

1190. How much communication is task-related?

1191. Were any strategies or activities unsuccessful?

1192. What skills did you need that were missing on this ThirdParty Management project?

1193. How many interest groups are stakeholders?

1194. What is the supplier dependency?

1195. Did the team work well together?

1196. What needs to be done over or differently?

1197. How was the ThirdParty Management project controlled?

1198. How well were ThirdParty Management project issues communicated throughout your involvement in the ThirdParty Management project?

1199. How timely was the training you received in preparation for the use of the product/service?

1200. What were the main sources of frustration in the ThirdParty Management project?

1201. What is your organizational ideology?

1202. What are the needs of the individuals?

1203. What are your lessons learned that you will keep in mind for the next ThirdParty Management project you participate in?

1204. Who managed most of the communication within the ThirdParty Management project?

1205. Did the ThirdParty Management project improve the team members reputations, skills, personal development?

Index